Ladies, First
Common Threads

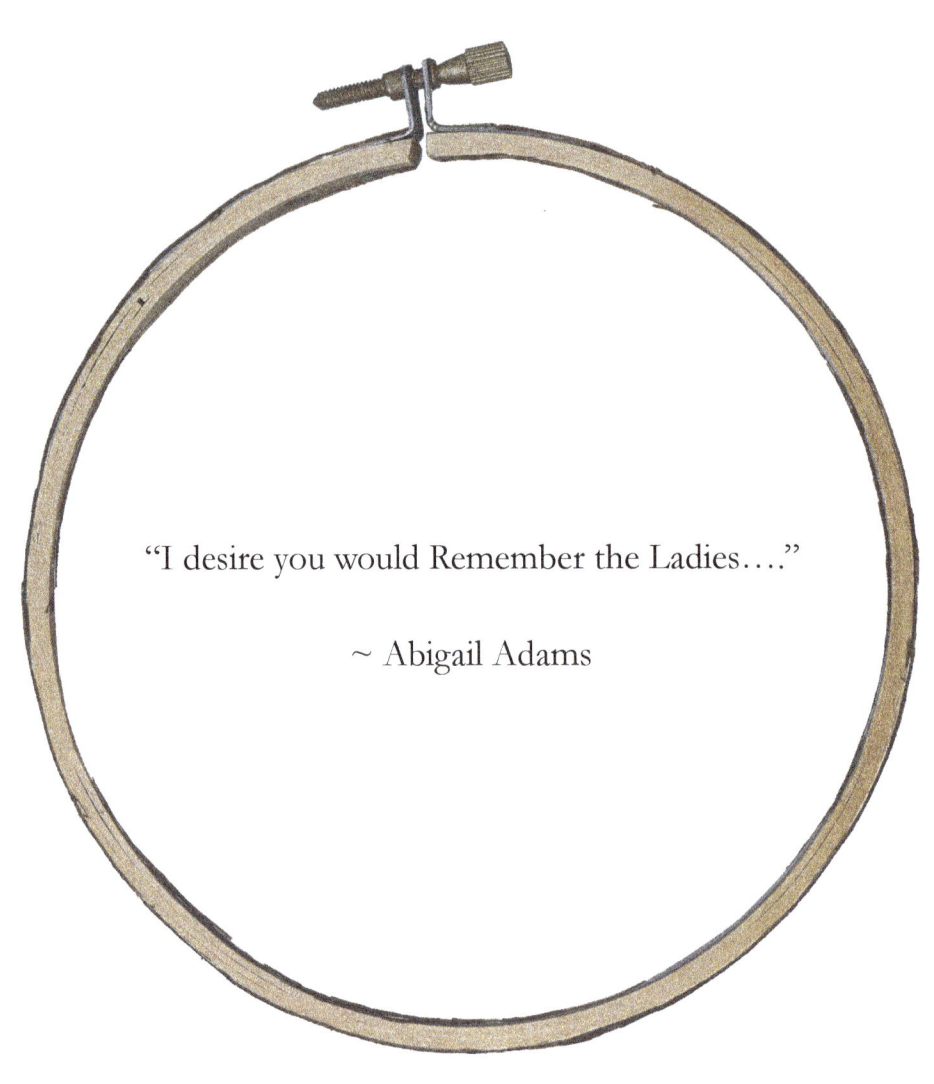

"I desire you would Remember the Ladies…."

~ Abigail Adams

Ladies, First
Common Threads

Debra Scala Giokas

Every year on the last Saturday in April,
National First Ladies Day commemorates
the first First Lady of the United States,
Martha Washington,
and all those who followed in her footsteps.
It's a day to recognize the role the first ladies
have played and continue to play in shaping America.

© 2022 by Debra Scala Giokas
Cover Art by Mary Ryan Reeves
All rights reserved. No part of this publication may be reproduced, transmitted, or stored in an information retrieval system in any form or by any means, electronic or mechanical, including photocopying, taping, and recording or otherwise without prior written permissions of the publisher.
ISBN 978-1-7367254-4-3

Chandelier Street
New York

In memory of my grandmothers,
and for my mom — my first lady,
and my husband, for making me his

How This Book Is Stitched Together...

To get you hooked on history,
this book unravels stories about
18 first ladies of the United States
who could knit, crochet,
embroider, quilt, cross-stitch or sew
(or even used a sewing machine a few times).

That's one of the common threads.

You'll find in each chapter,
a story, biography and then a "visit" section
where you can travel to learn more,
in both the virtual and real worlds.

These pages also contain a patchwork of images
that contribute to the fabric of American history,
collected from the helpful hands at work in our nation's
various libraries, museums and historic homes.

Special thanks to these curators, librarians and historians
for safeguarding the scrapbooks of America's story.
They are all mentioned in the acknowledgments,
which follow more fun facts about the first ladies.

Contents

Introduction	
Martha Dandrige Custis Washington	10
Abigail Smith Adams	18
Dolley Payne Todd Madison	24
Louisa Catherine Johnson Adams	30
Margaret Mackall Smith Taylor	36
Abigail Powers Fillmore	42
Eliza McCardle Johnson	48
Frances Clara Folsom Cleveland	54
Ida Saxton McKinley	62
Edith Kermit Carow Roosevelt	68
Helen Herron Taft	76
Edith Bolling Galt Wilson	82
Florence Mabel Kling Harding	88
Grace Anna Goodhue Coolidge	94
Lou Henry Hoover	100
Eleanor Roosevelt	108
Rosalynn Smith Carter	114
Barbara Pierce Bush	120
Afterword	128
First Lady Trivia	130
List of First Ladies	131
A White House Tradition	132
Acknowledgments	134
Bibliography	135

Introduction
Common Threads

My Grandma Rose knitted. My Grandma Lois crocheted. My mom embroidered beautiful pictures she framed. Over the years, I found my favorite needlework. I became skilled at crocheting. What does this have to do with the first ladies?

Well, one day in 2018 I happened upon the story of Ida Saxton McKinley's crocheted slippers, and I wondered if any other first ladies liked to count stitches, too. I thought it would be a fun way to touch history.

I set out to learn about first ladies who have some connection to yarn or threads, whether the needlework be crocheting, knitting, sewing or embroidery. I found 18. And I was hooked.

I learned about Grace Coolidge crocheting the blanket for the Lincoln bed, Eleanor Roosevelt knitting for the troops during World War II, and Eliza Johnson sewing and embroidering. I learned more about their lives…stories I had never known.

When I was in elementary school, we didn't cover the first ladies in our curriculum — only that Martha Washington was grandmotherly and Dolley Madison served ice cream.

My other education about our first ladies came with a trip to the Smithsonian National Museum of American History. I had admired their gowns. But there is more to these women than their clothes.

In my research, I was amazed at the lack of books on the shelves about these iconic women, as compared to the presidents. As one librarian told me, "We have books on the ones in the beginning and the current ones, but not much on the ones in the middle."

Ida McKinley helped me again. The First Ladies National Historic Site is located in her ancestral home in Canton, Ohio, and it was a great source

Ida McKinley's blue crocheted slippers. Courtesy of the First Ladies' Library

in helping me to stitch this book together. It consists of a library and a museum. This museum began with an idea from Mary Regula, the wife of an Ohio congressman. She believed girls "desperately needed role models." She once said, "Girls in particular get shortchanged. History books are written by men."

    I encountered more surprises and kindnesses along the way. The librarians and archivists at many of our nation's historic homes, national parks, and libraries were helpful and invaluable resources.

    In the beginning of my project, I had the privilege of reading Lou Henry Hoover's typed acceptance speech for an award for her research paper on mining. She was the first woman to earn a degree in geology from Stanford University. She was a knitter, too. First Lady Hoover stated that evening:

> But the one preeminent characteristic
> that went to accomplish it,
> the one of which I am really very proud,
> because I did not know before I possessed it,
> was perseverance. It was of necessity
> a very slow performance,
> comparable to the unravelling of
> a great tangle of knotted string.

Lou Henry Hoover reminded me about perseverance. She gave me the encouragement to "stick to it." As I began to untangle my knotted string and unravel these stories of some of our first ladies, I discovered more about their minds and hearts.

    And I became more determined in my belief that we should be learning about them, as much as our presidents. For in each case, the president would not have been the president he was without the first lady by his side. As Abigail Adams once said, "Remember the Ladies."

    These women were becoming my friends, as I invited myself into their lives. I smiled with them. I cried with them. I was inspired by them.

    I hope you enjoy reading about them, as much as I enjoyed writing about them.

    Think about the common threads that connect these women. Some include sacrifice, courage, and generosity of spirit. But there is plenty more for you to discover and discuss, and many places for you to visit to make history come alive.

    May these first ladies inspire you to become the person you were meant to be and to contribute something to our world too.

~ Debra Scala Giokas

How did the title "First Lady" begin?

It's difficult to pinpoint, as there are a few claims.

Initially, the President's wife was referred to as "Lady." Martha Washington was "Lady Washington." Dolley was referred to as Lady Presidentress.

In an 1877 article describing the inauguration of President Rutherford B. Hayes, Mary Clemmer Ames used the term "First Lady."

In 1911 in New York City, the term was popularized through a play about Dolley Madison entitled, "The First Lady of the Land."

It is also claimed that in 1830, it was used to refer to Martha Washington.

In addition, when Mary Todd Lincoln lived in the White House, the "New York Herald" and the "Sacramento Union" newspapers called her First Lady.

The term has remained ever since.

MARTHA DANDRIDGE CUSTIS WASHINGTON

Martha Washington Moves to the President's Mansion

Martha and George Washington never lived in the White House. When George was elected the first President of the United States in 1789, he and Martha moved to the nation's capital in New York City to live in the President's Mansion at 1 Cherry Street. The big brick mansion filled with beautiful furniture had living quarters, a private office for the president, and a business office.

Before Martha began her trip to New York, she sat alone in her bedroom at her home in Mount Vernon, Virginia. Martha used to sit alone for an hour every day. Nobody was allowed to bother her. She liked to meditate. She also thought about all the things she liked to do in her home like knitting, reading, and praying.

That day, Martha thought about her good memories at Mount Vernon. She remembered her dinner and dancing parties and the time George played the drums on the table with his fork and spoon. George was a great dancer of the Minuet, a popular ballroom dance at that time. After the American Revolutionary War ended, Martha threw parties for the brave soldiers.

Martha closed her eyes and began thinking about the other places at Mount Vernon too. The farm where she raised chickens, the garden where she grew vegetables, and the kitchen filled with smells of pancakes, butter and honey. Martha had memorized everything about her home.

New York, New York

She was sad that she had to leave, but she knew that George, now the President of the United States, needed her. Her country needed her too.

In a horse-drawn carriage, Martha left Mount Vernon for New York City. She rode up north with her nephew Robert Lewis and her 10-year-old granddaughter Nelly, and Little Wash, her 8-year-old grandson. Sadly, all of Martha and George's children had died, so they raised Nelly and Wash as their own.

Along their way to New York, people greeted them with cheers and celebrations. In Baltimore, fireworks burst into the night and people sang songs. When they reached Philadelphia, church bells rang, and soldiers fired a 13-gun salute in Martha's honor.

But the trip was not easy. One night, the carriage broke down, and the horses gave them trouble. Finally, 11 days later, George met them in New Jersey, and they took the president's boat to New York. When people saw the boat, they shouted, "God Bless Lady Washington!"

In New York City, a parade came down the streets to celebrate Martha's arrival, and soldiers fired another 13-gun-salute. Martha was excited to be the first lady, but she was also nervous.

New York was the U.S. capital between April 1789 and 1790. Alexander Hamilton and citizens suggested New York because of its hotels and restaurants that were needed for a capital city and for its location between northern and southern states.

Martha's New Role

What did a first lady do? Nobody had done it before. How could she show people that the new government was for the people and by the people? Martha thought about the parties and dinners she hosted at Mount Vernon for the troops during the American Revolution, and she had an idea. Martha would invite people to the Presidential Mansion.

And that's what she did. Martha began holding receptions called "levees" every Friday night. She invited congressmen, very important people from other countries, and community members.

Martha served coffee, tea, cake, and lemonade. She also served a new dessert called ice cream. George, who had bad teeth, liked it because it was soft.

Martha wore simple clothes made in New England factories. At Martha's receptions, George and Martha did not wear formal clothing because they did not want the American people to think that they were acting like the King and Queen of England and holding a royal court.

Even though Martha enjoyed the Presidential Mansion, she still missed Mount Vernon. She was not used to living in the city or being famous. Journalists followed her around and wrote about what she did every day like taking Nelly and Little Wash to the theater and museums. It was hard getting used to being the center of attention.

But Martha learned how to keep herself happy. She would say, "Keep yourself busy as a bee, cheerful as a cricket, and steady as a clock." Martha enjoyed sewing clothes, and she kept Nelly and Little Wash busy as bees, too. Nelly went to a school for young women. Martha hired a famous musician and artist to teach Nelly, and Nelly learned to play the harpsichord, paint, and draw. Martha spoiled Little Wash. He could do no wrong and got away with everything.

Before Martha could adjust to life in New York City, Congress voted to name the District of Columbia the nation's capital, which is known

Lady Washington's Reception
Smithsonian American Art Museum
SAAM-1966.48.58

as Washington D.C. George hired the French engineer Pierre Charles L'Enfant to build the new city, and slaves began building Martha and George's new house.

Although Martha and George were excited to finally have a permanent home, they would have to move to Philadelphia until the house was complete. Sadly, George's time as president ended before their new home in Washington D.C. was built, and they returned to Mount Vernon.

Martha was happy to be home again at Mount Vernon. She and George continued to host hundreds of visitors for dinner and overnight stays, and Martha still spent one hour alone each day. But Martha had changed. She would never forget her time as first lady. Martha did her part to help America succeed and forever influenced how future first ladies would act and behave. Martha was a true American hero.

George Washington and His Family
Smithsonian American Art Museum SAAM-1966.48.56

Martha Washington's Penn Treaty Quilt
(c. 1790 -1802) Cotton and Linen, 100 3/4 in. x 100 3/4 in.
Courtesy of the Mount Vernon Ladies' Association

One of the many ways Martha Washington kept herself "busy as a bee" was to do needlework. Martha made quilts. Martha also loved to sew and made bags for buttons, chair cushions and footstools.

Martha Washington's Needle Book and Pin Cushion
Courtesy of the Mount Vernon Ladies' Association

LEFT AND BELOW:

Needle Book

Martha Washington is believed to have made this needle book. It is embroidered and intended to be hung from the waistband by the ribbon. The needle book stored needles in the layers of wool between its stiff walls. By applying pressure on either side of the "mouth," the object was opened. Then the needle worker could push in or take out pins.

ABOVE:

Pin Cushion

Martha Washington is believed to have embroidered this elegant pincushion (above) during the winter encampment at Valley Forge, as a present for the daughter of her host. The colorful silk is wrapped in silver thread. It is beautiful and functional, which is characteristic of Martha's work. It shows no signs of use, though, as one descendant said that it was treated with "reverential care."

Martha Washington's Quilt Top
(c. 1800 - 1802), Cotton, 100 in. × 97 1/2 in.
Courtesy of the Mount Vernon Ladies' Association

During the American Revolution, Martha travelled in the winters to be with George. She stayed on the front lines and knitted socks for the troops, sewed their uniforms, and raised money for supplies. Martha also nursed wounded soldiers. She hosted dinner parties to fill their bellies and cheer them up.

MARTHA DANDRIDGE CUSTIS WASHINGTON
Lady Washington (1789 – 1797)

Martha Washington
Currier & Ives lithograph
Library of Congress cph.3b51147

Miniature of Martha

John Wollaston painted this portrait of Martha in 1757, the year her first husband died. She was 26 years old. In 1859, John Cheney engraved the portrait and then painted this miniature, based on his own engraving.

Smithsonian American Art Museum
SAAM-1999.27.6

Martha Dandridge Custis Washington was born on June 2, 1731 on Chestnut Grove Plantation near Williamsburg, Virginia. Her parents were John Dandridge and Frances Jones Dandridge. She did not attend school, but she read the Bible and Gothic novels. Her mother taught her how to sew and maintain a household. Her nickname was Patsy.

At 19, she married 38-year-old Daniel Parke Custis. He died in 1757, and Martha became the wealthiest woman in Virginia. She had 17,500 acres of land, but kept 300 enslaved people to take care of it.

Martha had four children: Daniel Custis, Frances Custis, John (Jacky) Custis, and Martha (Patsy) Custis.

Colonel George Washington was the commander of the Virginia forces during the French and Indian War.

Martha married George on January 6, 1759 at her home in New Kent County. She was 5 feet tall and a beautiful brunette. She wore a gown made of heavy gold fabric, and she wore purple satin slippers. George was 6 feet 2 inches tall. He had auburn hair and blue eyes. He was athletic and a great ballroom dancer. No pictures exist of George Washington before the age of 40.

Martha's children Jacky and Patsy were still alive at that time. They moved to Mount Vernon in the spring of 1759. George never had biological children. He raised Jacky and Patsy as his own. Patsy died of a seizure at 17, and Jacky was killed during the Revolutionary War.

The American people loved Martha. They knew she sacrificed like her husband during the American Revolution which took place between 1765 and 1783. Martha endured the cold winter at Valley Forge where 2,500 soldiers had died. Between April 1775 and December 1783, Martha was with George for almost half the time he was away from home. Before she made her first trip, however, she had to get an injection to fight smallpox.

Martha managed the daily operations at Mount Vernon and even held a clinic at Mount Vernon in 1777 so people could get their smallpox injection, too.

When George and Martha moved to New York, they lived in the first presidential mansion which was once called the Samuel Osgood House. The home also included the office of the Executive, a tradition that continues to this day. The Osgood House was demolished in 1856. A plaque marks its location at an approach to the Brooklyn Bridge.

In 1798 alone, the couple entertained more than 650 guests at Mount Vernon.

Martha was a private person. After George died on December 14, 1799, Martha locked their bedroom. She moved upstairs to the Garret bedroom. She visited her husband's tomb every day on the property.

She also burned all of his letters. Her granddaughter Nelly found two letters in her desk. One letter describes George buying cotton material for dresses. Historians believe more letters exist, and they are looking for them.

Eleanor "Nelly" Parke Custis (known as "Nelly") was the youngest of Martha Washington's three granddaughters. Her parents were John ("Jacky") Parke Custis and Eleanor Calvert.

Nelly married George Washington's nephew, Lawrence Lewis. She had her first child 17 days before George died. Throughout her life, Nelly Parke Custis Lewis maintained George and Martha's legacy. George Washington Parke Custis (known as "Wash") was Nelly's brother and the youngest grandchild.

One of his accomplishments is restoring a mansion called Arlington House. Arlington House is a shrine to George Washington, and you can see it at Arlington National Cemetery in Washington D.C.

VISIT:

**Mount Vernon
3200 Mount Vernon
Memorial Highway
Mount Vernon, VA 22121**

mountvernon.org

George and Martha's Burial Site
Courtesy of the Author

Mount Vernon is the name of George and Martha Washington's home. People have been visiting this large plantation since 1860, making it the most popular historic estate in America.

Courtesy of the Mount Vernon Ladies' Association

ABIGAIL SMITH ADAMS

Dearest Friend and Political Partner

On November 16, 1800, Abigail Adams left the temporary Executive Mansion in Philadelphia and set out for Washington D.C., the new capital of the United States. Abigail and her husband, President John Adams, would be the first family to move into the White House, where they would live for the rest of President Adams's term.

When Abigail first saw the White House, she did not like it. She told her daughter that it was a "great castle." Washington D.C. was not the city she envisioned either, as there were many muddy roads. The White House was built on a swamp. She saw the slaves painting, plastering, and carting building materials, and that made her angry. Abigail thought slavery was wrong and should not be allowed. Abigail was not afraid to voice her opinion on anything and everything.

In those days, it was highly unusual for a woman to speak her mind. Abigail's father and her husband both called her "saucy" because she was full of spunk.

Abigail stepped into her first lady shoes and went to work. Because the White House was still a work in progress and Abigail was a practical person, she had her laundry hung in the unfinished East Room that was intended for entertaining guests.

Abigail had another laundry list – of what she knew should be done.

Abigail was not afraid to voice her opinion on anything and everything.

Because she argued passionately for her beliefs, people called her Mrs. President.

Abigail thought slavery was wrong.

Abolish slavery!
Women to own property!
Married women are not the property of men!
Educate women, too!
Women must have equal representation!

She wrote a famous letter to John on March 31, 1776. She asked him to "remember the ladies." She also warned him that if the government didn't treat women fairly, women would rebel.

In another letter to him on August 14, 1776, Abigail said that if the country wants to have heroes, then women should be educated, too.

Abigail also wrote to John about military strategy, politics, the economy, family, and health. Because she argued so passionately for her beliefs, people called her Mrs. President.

Hollow-cut Silhouette

The artist Raphaelle Peale stayed with the Adamses in October 1804. He was traveling along the east coast in search of sitters for profile portraits. That is when this silhouette was probably made. Later in 1809, John Quincy Adams added the inscription and date when he grouped a number of family members' silhouettes together in one frame.

National Portrait Gallery, Smithsonian Institution NPG.78.282

Abigail's Sewing Pocket

Courtesy of the Massachusetts Historical Association

"All old ladies wore these under pockets & carried their keys in them."

~ Elizabeth Coombs Adams

This dimity pocket was worn by Abigail Adams in the late 18th or early 19th century.

An accompanying note by Abigail's granddaughter, Elizabeth Coombs Adams, reads: "All old ladies wore these under pockets & carried their keys in them." The pocket is 14 inches long and would have been tied above her petticoat and under her skirt.

Abigail believed strongly that everyone should have freedom, education, and property. She didn't know if she had the patience expected from a first lady to watch her every word and not rock the boat. In Washington D.C., changes to the laws happened slowly. Abigail asked her good friend Martha Washington for advice, and Martha replied, "You know inside yourself how to behave."

Like Martha, Abigail missed her husband's inauguration. Abigail couldn't go to Philadelphia because she was taking care of family matters on the farm in Braintree, Massachusetts. Two weeks later on March 4, 1797, John wrote, "I never wanted your advice and assistance more in my life."

Even though they weren't in the same place all of the time, John and Abigail were together through letters. She had been giving him her opinions in letters since they began dating.

On more occasions than she'd care to remember, John Adams left his dearest friend – that's how he addressed Abigail – so that he could take care of the country. John, the Harvard-educated lawyer turned politician, could not have devoted his time to public service without her.

Through it all, Abigail took care of five children, taught them at home, and tended the farm. When others were afraid to, she invested in risky bonds during the American Revolution and made a good return.

Abigail lived through a smallpox epidemic and lost a child at birth. She also watched the first battle of the American Revolution from Penn's Hill with her children about a half mile from her home, and she cared for soldiers. With all of this responsibility on the home front and no formal education, Abigail read everything she could get her hands on and kept thinking big ideas.

She was the ultimate multitasker and the original super mom. John Adams wouldn't have accomplished what he did without Abigail's brilliant advice.

President John Adams was not elected to a second term. The couple returned to Massachusetts in 1801. This was a marriage of equals, even though America was not ready to recognize it. Abigail wanted America to recognize women as equal to men.

On June 5, 1809, John Adams wrote a letter to Abigail's sister, Elizabeth Smith Shaw Peabody. He said, "I have always wished to impress upon the minds of my children that no man ever prospered in the world without the consent and cooperation of his wife."

Abigail Adams understood girl power. She reminded us to remember the ladies, and she will always be unforgettable.

Abigail knew how to sew and quilt and made practical items.
She wrote to John Adams on October 25, 1775 and asked him to
"remember my other bundle of pins."

Most importantly, in her famous letter on March 31, 1776,
Abigail asked John to "remember the ladies."

President John Quincy Adams's youngest son, Charles Frances Adams,
published the couple's letters. There are more than 1,160 letters.

Sampler Embroidered by Abigail Adams

This sampler includes a house, a peacock, urns of flowers, birds, and Adam and Eve with the Tree of Knowledge. A geometric border surrounds three sides, and a strawberry vine borders all four. At the top is the date "1789, and at the bottom is the inscription, "Abigail Adams her work New York."

Cooper Hewitt, Smithsonian Design Museum Collection, Bequest of Mrs. Henry E. Coe 1941-69-243

ABIGAIL SMITH ADAMS
2nd First Lady (1797 – 1801)
1st Second Lady and Mother of 6th President

Abigail Adams
Photo by Chester A. Lawrence,
Dorchester, Massachusetts,
of painting by Gilbert Stuart.
Library of Congress cph.3b04614

Abigail Smith Adams was born to the Reverend William Smith and Elizabeth Quincy Smith in Weymouth, Massachusetts on November 22, 1744. Some biographers cite November 11. That date is under an old calendar system by Julius Caesar.

Abigail's grandmother read to her, and Abigail loved to learn. She was brilliant and read books in her father's library. He was a minister in the Congregational Church.

She married John Adams on October 25, 1764. She was 19, and he was 28. They were married for 54 years.

They had six children. One child, Elizabeth, died at birth. Abigail (Nabby) Amelia died at the age of 48 from breast cancer. Susanna died at the age of two from an unknown childhood disease. Charles, an alcoholic, died at the age of 30. Thomas Boylston became a lawyer.

John Quincy, their second child and eldest son, became the 6th President of the United States.

Abigail was not alive to see John Quincy become president. She is one of two women to be wife and mother to two presidents. (The other is Barbara Bush).

Abigail and John had a wonderful marriage. She always wore a locket that he gave her. Sometimes John did not write as often. He didn't write personal things because he thought the British might take his letters. This bothered Abigail. She needed his encouragement back home. During the Revolutionary War, Abigail asked George Washington to deliver by hand a letter to John.

In letters, Abigail sometimes referred to herself as Portia, who was the wife of Brutus. Brutus killed Julius Caesar. Portia is a powerful symbol of loyalty.

During the American Revolution, John Adams served as United States Minister to France and then England. Abigail remained in Massachusetts but then later joined him.

She did not approve of French fashion. Her style was puritanical or simple. Puritans were strict in their religious beliefs. She also had strong political beliefs.

John Adams beat Thomas Jefferson by a narrow margin, and Jefferson became his vice president. Back then, the losing candidate became the vice president.

Abigail was the first First Lady to live in the Executive Mansion, later called the White House, in Washington D.C. She was also the first second lady, which is the title given to spouses of the vice president. She is one of two women to be wife and mother to two presidents. (The other is Barbara Bush.)

When Adams ran for re-election, Jefferson won. For years, Abigail held a grudge against Thomas Jefferson because he did not agree with Adams's decision to keep peace with France.

The Adamses' home was in Braintree, Massachusetts. When John became Vice President, they lived in New York which was the U.S. capital. Then they lived in Philadelphia when the U.S. capital moved to Philadelphia and for the reminder of John's vice presidency.

In the Executive Mansion in Philadelphia, Abigail hosted two receptions a week.

Abigail died at her home on October 28, 1818 at the age of 73 from typhoid fever. John survived her by 8 years and lived to the age of 90.

John Adams and Thomas Jefferson died on July 4, 1826, a few hours apart and 50 years after signing the Declaration of Independence.

VISIT:

**The Adams National Historic Site
133 Franklin St.
Quincy, MA 02169**

It contains 11 historic structures.

nps.gov/adams

**Abigail Adams Birthplace
180 Norton St.
Weymouth, MA 02191**

abigailadamsbirthplace.com

Birthplace of John Quincy Adams
Abigail also wrote many of her famous letters to her husband from this farm at the foot of Penn's Hill.

Courtesy of the National Park Service, Adams National Historic Park

DOLLEY PAYNE TODD MADISON

Dolley Takes Command

First Lady Dolley Madison was home at the White House on August 22, 1814. Her husband, President James Madison, was not with her. He was with his army in Maryland because the United States and Great Britain were fighting the War of 1812, which is also known as the "Second War of Independence."

President Madison heard about Britain's plans to burn down the White House and kidnap Dolley. The British wanted to make Dolley a prisoner of war and parade her down the streets of London. When President Madison found out, he sent a message to Dolley and told her to leave right away.

Sociable and Brave

The British armed forces wanted to target Dolley because she was popular and outspoken. She made speeches on behalf of James and threw parties called "squeezes" that everyone in Washington D.C. wanted to attend. Before James was elected President, Dolley's parties were so popular that she was named the "unofficial" First Lady to President Thomas Jefferson, the third President of the United States whose wife Martha had died 19 years before his presidency.

Why were Dolley's parties so popular? She knew how to decorate and how to set a beautiful table with elegant silverware. She invited all kinds of people and played music, and always carried a book with her so she would have something other than politics to talk about with her guests. Dolley was a leader in fashion, especially French designs. She wore a turban on her head so her guests could find her. Dolley also knew how to feed her guests and served all kinds of special foods including ice cream. Thomas Jefferson gave her the recipe. Her favorite? Oyster ice cream. Yes, oyster!

Once James Madison was elected president, Dolley continued to host her parties, and when the papers wrote stories about her fun parties, everyone in the country wanted to attend.

When Dolley received the message, she didn't panic. While everyone in Washington D.C. evacuated, Dolley stayed. Dolley was courageous.

Dolley grabbed an original copy of the Declaration of Independence. She also took the silverware, and she ripped the red velvet drapes from the window.

Dolley instructed a 15-year-old enslaved servant named Paul Jennings who was the doorkeeper and gardener to remove the portrait of President George Washington, the one painted by the famous

Dolley wore a turban on her head so her guests could find her, and she always carried a book with her so she would have something else to talk about besides politics.

Dolley threw parties called "squeezes."

Dolley Madison with her signature turban c.1848

Courtesy of the Greensboro History Museum

Thanks to Dolley Madison, the oil painting of George Washington is still in the White House. Legend says that she later sewed her famous red velvet dress out of the White House's drapes she kept the night the White House burned down, but it has not been proven.

artist of that time, Gilbert Stuart. Then it was sent to New York for safekeeping.

Dolley saved what she could and fled to safety.

On August 24, the British burned the U.S. Capitol. Strangely, before they torched the White House, they feasted on an elegant dinner with several kinds of wine and toasted Lady Madison in her absence.

Then the unimaginable happened.

It started to rain and thunder. Tornado-like conditions blew roofs off the Post Office and the Patent Office Building. A bridge over the Potomac River buckled. Two canons flew off the ground. Houses tossed around. The storm lasted for two hours, and the heavy rains put out the fires. The British troops finally had to leave.

People lost their homes during The War of 1812, and James and Dolley Madison returned to no home too. The White House had burned down. Homeless people, widows, and orphans filled the streets. James and Dolley rented a home nearby and had lots of work to do.

Rebuilding The White House and Washington D.C.

Although many urged President Madison to move the White House to a safer place, Dolley insisted that they stay and rebuild both the White House and Washington D.C., which would become a national symbol. Dolley helped people heal their broken hearts.

When Marcia Van Ness and Elizabeth Riley Brown had asked Dolley to help orphans in Washington D.C., she said yes. Marcia was the wife of a former New York congressman, and Brown was the wife of the pastor of the First Baptist Church in Washington.

Dolley agreed with their idea to create the Washington Female Orphan Asylum, later called the Washington City Orphan Asylum.

Dolley Madison's red velvet gown.

Courtesy Greensboro History Museum

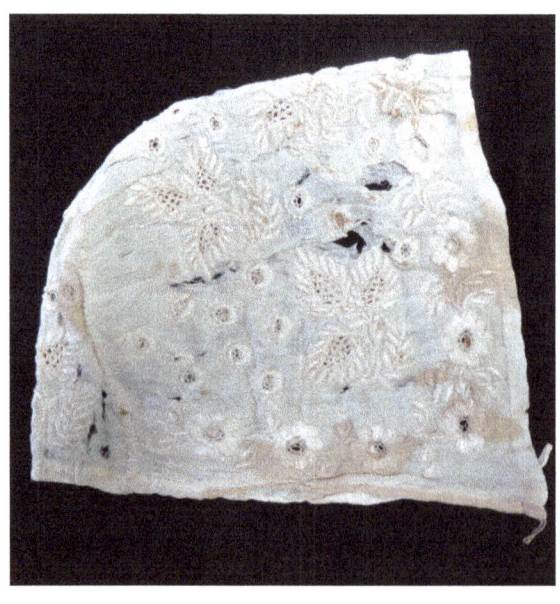

Baby Cap
*Courtesy of
The James Madison Museum
of Orange County Heritage*

The orphanage would house, clothe, feed, and educate needy children. The orphanage helped primarily girls from Washington D.C. and its surrounding areas.

Dolley donated $20 and a cow so the children could get milk. She even sewed clothes for them.

Dolley's charming ways raised awareness for the orphanage and she was elected its first Directress. Dolley became the first First Lady to get involved with a public works project.

First Lady Dolley Madison is more known for her bravery in saving the portrait of George Washington than she is for her work with the orphanage.

Indeed, her heart full of courage and compassion elevated the role of the first lady in American history. She always had a kind word and a smile. People grew to love this vivacious woman more and more with each passing year.

At a New Year's Eve Party in 1838, a senator from Kentucky named Henry Clay summed it up best, "Everybody loves Mrs. Madison."

To this she answered, "Mr. Clay, I love everybody."

Dolley's charming ways raised awareness for the orphanage and she was elected its first Directress. Dolley became the first First Lady to get involved with a public works project.

The Washington Female Orphan Asylum still exists today but is now called the Hillcrest Children's Center. It's no longer an orphanage but helps people who are mentally ill.

Dolley Madison gifted baby caps she knitted.

The Baby Cap knitted and interwoven with ribbons made by Dolley as a gift for Reuben and Phoebe Butler Newman on the birth of their son, James Butler Newman in 1806. Theodore Scott, Jr. had it framed with monetary assistance from Barbara Dinwiddie and her sister, Mrs. W.B. Perkins of Fork Union.

Courtesy of The James Madison Museum of Orange County Heritage

DOLLEY PAYNE TODD MADISON
4th First Lady (1809 – 1817)

Dolley Madison
Photograph of a painting by Gilbert Stuart at the Pennsylvania Academy of the Fine Arts.
Library of Congress
det.4a26107

Dolley Madison
By William S. Elwel (1848)
The portrait offers a glimpse of the aging Mrs. Madison, described by the artist in his diary as "a very Estimable lady-kind & obliging-one of the Old School."

National Portrait Galleery
Smithsonian Institution NPG.74.6

Dolley Payne Todd Madison was born on May 20, 1768 in Guilford County, North Carolina. When her father freed his slaves and sold the farm in Virginia, her family moved to Philadelphia to set up a business and it unfortunately failed.

After Dolley's father died, her mother opened a boardinghouse.

At that time, women could not own property if they were married. They were considered the property of their husband.

Like her parents, Dolley was a Quaker. She married John Todd, a lawyer and a Quaker, in 1790. The couple had two sons, John Payne Todd and William Temple Todd. Her husband, in-laws, and her newborn baby William died from yellow fever. Dolley almost died too.

She was left a widow at 25 with a young son, John, to raise. She helped out her mom at the boardinghouse. She was so pretty and popular that men would wait outside her home to greet her, sometimes 10 at a time.

About a year later, Aaron Burr, Vice President to Thomas Jefferson, introduced Dolley to James Madison, a successful politician who was called the "Father of the Constitution" at that time. A long-time bachelor, he was 17 years older than Dolley. After a few months, they were married on September 15, 1794.

At Madison's inauguration, she wore an ivory gown with a long train and a purple bonnet topped with feathers. After marrying Madison, she was officially shunned from the Quaker faith (as he was not one), but she kept her childhood friends and enjoyed wearing fashionable clothing.

The War of 1812 was fought on land in North America and at sea and ended when the peace treaty, called the Treaty of Ghent, was ratified on February 16, 1815 by consent of Congress and executed with President Madison's signature.

During the War, a lawyer by the name of Francis Scott Key penned a poem called "Defence of Fort McHenry," which put to music later became the national anthem, "The Star-Spangled Banner" in 1931.

The portrait of George Washington was returned in 1817 and still hangs in the White House today.

The couple retired to Montpelier, their Virginia estate. They experienced financial hardships because of the cost of maintaining an enslaved labor force, draughts and poor crops and many unexpected visitors. After her husband's death, Dolley left her son Payne in charge of the estate and his gambling habits bankrupted Montpelier.

So special and loved was Dolley that Congress stepped in and provided a trust of $25,000, and she lived off the interest. Congress also honored Dolley Madison with her own seat, and she watched the debates. This was a rare privilege. As a woman, Dolley was never permitted to vote.

In 1837, Dolley moved out of Montpelier. She returned to a home the Madisons owned on Lafayette Square, across from the White House. People in Washington D.C. invited her to all the parties. They looked after her and wanted to be with her. Dolley had a lot of friends.

First Lady Dolley Madison died on July 12, 1849. Four days later, more than 3,000 people were present at the largest funeral procession in Washington D.C. up until that time. Foreign dignitaries, members of Congress and people from all economic classes watched her bronze casket accompanied by 48-horse drawn carriages. Enslaved servants were on one of those carriages. They traveled from St. John's Church to the Congressional Cemetery where she was temporarily buried. Everyone loved her.

In 1857, Dolley was finally brought home to Montpelier as she had wished.

The Dolly (spelled without the e) Madison Bakery was started in 1937. The name was used for a popular ice cream brand, with a logo of the silhouette of Dolley Madison, which sold in the United States during the mid-20th century.

Dolley Madison
in her youth, an ivory portrait.
Courtesy of the James Madison Museum of Orange County Heritage

James Madison Museum of Orange County Heritage
Courtesy of The James Madison Museum of Orange County Heritage

VISIT:

**The Montpelier Estate
13384 Laundry Road
Montpelier Station, VA 22960**

montpelier-vt.org

It is a memorial to James Madison and the enslaved community.

**The James Madison Museum of Orange County Heritage
129 Caroline Street
Orange, VA 22960**

thejamesmadisonmuseum.net

Learn more about President James Madison, First Lady Dolley Madison, President Zachary Taylor and Orange County. Its "Madison Room" features personal possessions and documents of James and Dolley Madison.

LOUISA CATHERINE JOHNSON ADAMS

A Journey of Her Own

Before he became President of the United States, John Quincy Adams was a foreign diplomat. His wife, Louisa, born in England, was well-traveled and could speak many languages. But she never expected what John would ask of her during the cold winter of 1815.

John Quincy served as the Minister Plenipotentiary to Russia, the name for a position ranked right below an ambassador. John and Louisa were living in Russia when President James Madison asked John to go to France and negotiate a treaty to end the War of 1812 with Britain. Louisa stayed in Russia to watch their children.

After one year of being apart and when the Treaty of Ghent was signed, John sent for Louisa. He asked her to sell their property in St. Petersburg, Russia and travel to Paris, France.

On her 40th birthday, Louisa and her 7-year-old son, Charles, and some servants set out in a Russian-style carriage. Louisa's 1-year-old daughter had died, and this was still a difficult time for her. But she couldn't wait to be with John.

Her Trip to Paris

Louisa's journey of 2,000 miles in winter weather was not an easy one. During the course of 40 days, her carriage broke down, and she had to make her way through roads filled with wounded and dead soldiers because France was at war with Russia. Even though the French Emperor Napoleon Bonaparte had been captured and exiled to the island of Elba off the coast of Italy, he had escaped in 1815.

That's when Louisa happened to be traveling in France. Napoleon was Emperor again and on a rampage during a time known as The One Hundred Days War.

When the French soldiers saw her Russian-style coach, they stopped her. They wanted to kill her. Louisa had to figure out a way to protect herself, her son, and the others on board the coach. She bravely waved her handkerchief and yelled out in French, "Vivé Napoleon!"

The soldiers had heard a rumor that she may have been Napoleon's sister and when Louisa spoke in French, they believed it to be true. She was allowed to go on, and the group traveled safely to John in Paris.

John Quincy Adams relied on Louisa's help, 10 years later, to accomplish another huge task. He wanted to be President of the United States like his father John Adams.

Not only was Louisa courageous, but she was also beautiful, talented, and charming. She could sing and play the harp like an angel, and she had danced with kings such as Tsar Alexander I of Russia. In the days before presidential campaigns, Louisa figured out a way to make her shy husband popular.

She hosted a ball and invited Andrew Jackson, a national war hero. Jackson had defeated the British in the Battle of New Orleans during the War of 1812, almost 10 years before. Next to George Washington, Jackson was the country's favorite.

The newspapers called it the "Jackson Ball." They wrote about Louisa's gorgeous gown and how Andrew Jackson walked around the crowds with Louisa on his arm. Just as Louisa had hoped for, it was standing room only and the social event of the year!

Louisa's hard work paid off. The election was close, however, and the House of Representatives had to decide. John Quincy Adams emerged as President of the United States in 1824.

Louisa's White House

But White House life was not what First Lady Louisa Adams had expected. She called it the "Palace" because that's the impression people had of the White House. She knew the inside story and

The White House was rebuilt in 1817 after it burned down during the War of 1812, but when Louisa moved in, it was still a work in progress.

Louisa started this bedspread in 1835 and finished it in 1837. It was exhibited in 1837.
Courtesy of the National Park Service, Adams National Historic Park

called it a "half-finished barn." To set the record straight, she opened the White House doors. People saw the cracks in the walls, the bare fixtures, and the tired-looking furniture.

Like the "Palace" on the outside, Louisa started showing cracks on her inside. She was sad like the French queens and duchesses that she read about in her many books. She ate a lot of chocolate to make herself feel better. She was a chocaholic!

The couple didn't go out much anymore, and they entertained less and less. In the unfinished East Room, John Quincy kept a pet alligator in the bathtub, a gift from The Marquis de Lafayette who was a French aristocrat, and this scared many guests away.

To keep herself busy, Louisa raised silkworms on the mulberry trees so she could spin her own silk. She sewed many of her beautiful

dresses and kept her sewing items in a box shaped like a harpsichord.

She also picked up her pen and wrote letters, stories, poems, and plays, and she composed music.

At a time when men did not value women as equals and expect them to voice their opinions or write about them, Louisa bravely wrote down her thoughts and feelings. She wrote a memoir called a "Record of A Life, dated May 15, 1852." "Someday or other," she wrote, "my children may be amused with it."

Later on, she also wrote a book about her courageous journey in wintertime called "Narrative of a Journey from Russia to France, 1815."

Abigail Adams, her mother-in-law, also came to admire Louisa for her courageous journey. Louisa began reading the letters of Abigail Adams, and Louisa really appreciated Abigail more than ever before. Louisa called Abigail "the guiding planet around which all revolved." Women should not be forgotten! And Louisa agreed.

Though Louisa's memoirs were not published in her lifetime, Louisa is the first First Lady to have written a memoir while in the White House.

On June 23, 1828, John Quincy wrote, "She is winding silk from several hundred silkworms that she had been rearing."

Louisa is the first First Lady to have written a memoir while in the White House.

Like Dolley Madison, Louisa worked with the Washington Female Orphan Asylum.

Louisa's harpsichord sewing box.
Courtesy of the National Park Service, Adams National Historic Park

LOUISA CATHERINE JOHNSON ADAMS
6th First Lady (1825 – 1829)

Louisa Adams

Published in: The ladies of the White House, or, In the home of the Presidents / Laura Carter Holloway Langford. Philadelphia: Bradley, Garretson & Co., 1883, facing p. 238.
Library of Congress cph.3a16702

Louisa loved chocolate!

Louisa Adams

The artist Charles Bird King painted Louisa's portrait around 1824. She is elegantly dressed and plays the harp. The title on the music sheet reads "Oh! Say Not Woman's Heart Is Bought." King was detail-oriented and copied the lettering exactly as it appeared.

Smithsonian American Art Museum
1950.6.5

Louisa Catherine Johnson Adams was born in London, England on February 12, 1775. Her father, Joshua Johnson, was a merchant from Maryland and the United States consul in London. Her mother Catherine Nuth was British. Louisa was the second daughter and had five sisters and one brother: Ann "Nancy," Caroline, Harriet, Catherine, Elizabeth, and Thomas.

The family lived in a large house on Cooper's Row and had 11 servants. John Quincy Adams first met her when he was in England on a diplomatic mission.

Louisa and John married at the parish church of All Hallows-by-the-Tower on July 26, 1797 after a few postponements. John Quincy was 30, and she was 22. John Adams was vice president at that time. Louisa's father became bankrupt a few weeks after the wedding. He died in 1802. Her mother died in 1811.

Louisa had attended a convent school in France for years which introduced her to Catholicism. Her family had lived in Nantes France from 1778 until 1783. Louisa spoke French fluently. She learned how to read, write, embroider, and sew.

Later, Louisa became Episcopalian, and her faith grew stronger throughout her life. She often quoted passages from the Bible in her writings.

In addition to "Record of a Life," Louisa wrote a "Life of a Nobody" and "Narrative of a Journey from Russia to France, 1815" and an autobiographical play called "The Metropolitan Kaleidoscope." The two main characters are based on herself and John Quincy.

When John Adams became President, he appointed his son as American Minister to Prussia (Germany and Poland). King Frederick III and Queen Louisa liked Louisa Adams very much. She lived abroad with John Quincy in Berlin, St. Petersburg, and London.

When Louisa first came to America in 1801, she later wrote in her journal about meeting the Adams family: "Had I stepped into Noah's Ark, I do not think I could have been more utterly astonished."

John Quincy Adams served in the Senate from 1803 until 1808. They had three sons: George Washington; John, Jr.; and Charles Francis.

When James Madison became President in 1808, he appointed John Quincy as Minister Plenipotentiary to Russia. John Quincy accepted without even telling Louisa.

She traveled to Russia, at the age of 40, with Charles, the youngest son. Their daughter Louisa Catherine Adams II was born in

August of 1811, died a year later in September of 1812, and was buried in St. Petersburg, Russia.

Louisa was most happy living in England in a cottage with her husband and three sons. Then President Monroe appointed John Quincy to his cabinet, and Louisa and John moved back to Washington D.C. and lived on F Street.

John Quincy did not get re-elected, but his retirement didn't last long. He was elected a congressman in 1830 and served for 17 years. He was concerned with the abolitionist movement and women's rights. Louisa also worked on those issues, as she read the letters that Abigail and John had written to each other.

Her son George Washington Adams became a lawyer, and it is believed that he committed suicide by walking off a ship in 1829. John Adams II became a presidential aide and died at 31. Her youngest, Charles Francis Adams, became a diplomat, public official, and author.

In her later years, although she never liked the cold New England winters, Louisa made the Quincy house in Massachusetts her own, with furniture from Russia and England. She kept her sketches and small leather-bound books with her writings in her secretary desk near a small bookshelf.

On February 21, 1848, John Quincy Adams suffered a stroke at his desk in the House of Representatives. He died two days later in the Capitol. Although they did not have a smooth relationship, they had been married for 51 years.

That following spring, Louisa suffered a stroke and died on May 15, 1852. President Millard Fillmore attended Louisa's funeral, as did many high-ranking officials. This was the first time that Congress adjourned to honor a woman.

Louisa is buried with John Quincy Adams and President John Adams and First Lady Abigail Adams in the United First Parish Church in Quincy Massachusetts.

Louisa Adams was the first First Lady to be born outside of the United States and the only one until 192 years later when First Lady Melania Trump entered the White House.

Hollow-cut Silhouette

**Louisa Catherine Adams
By artist Henry Williams, 1809**
*National Portrait Gallery,
Smithsonian Institution*
S/NPG.78.209

Birthplace of John Quincy Adams

*Courtesy of the National Park Service,
Adams National Historic Park*

VISIT:

**The Adams
National Historic Site
133 Franklin St.
Quincy, MA 02169**

**It contains 11
historic structures.**

nps.gov/adams

MARGARET MACKALL SMITH TAYLOR

Courtesy of First Ladies' Library

A Devoted Army Wife

President Zachary Taylor once said about his wife, "Margaret is as much a solider as I ever was." When Margaret, nicknamed Peggy, fell in love with Lieutenant Zachary Taylor at the age of 21, her life changed forever. They married on June 25, 1810 in a double log cabin in Kentucky. And then she followed him on the frontier for almost 40 years, and at times she rode horseback to do so.

Peggy made their loving home in forts, tents, and log cabins. They lived in many places from the Florida Everglades to Fort Crawford in Wisconsin to the Jefferson Barracks of Missouri. She planted vegetables, skimmed milk, made butter, and even raised chickens. At one time at Fort Knox in Indiana, she was the only woman among 46 men. In Tampa, Florida, she served as a nurse in the army hospital.

Zachary knew this life was tough on Peggy. Peggy was lonely because she had sent her children away to live with relatives to spare them from frontier life and to earn a fine education. Zachary once wrote to his brother because he was worried about Peggy, "Peggy says if you come over, you must bring her some cotton for knitting which she wants mother to have spun for her."

The Legend

More than anything else, Peggy only wanted her husband to return safely from war. Legend says that she prayed for her husband's safety in exchange for her promise to be home and not attend any public functions or parties. General Zachary Taylor became a military war hero in the Mexican-American War, and his popularity won him the presidency in 1848.

On the frontier for 40 years, Peggy took care of the farm, nursed soldiers, and knitted to help with loneliness.

President Zachary Taylor said about his wife, "Margaret was as much a soldier as I ever was."

Zachary Taylor at Walnut Springs

One of President James Polk's objectives was to purchase California from Mexico. He sent the American Army to the Rio Grande. When Congress declared war on Mexico, General Zachary Taylor, a 40-year veteran, led the army to victory in Monterey and Buena Vista. People heard about his victories and that made Taylor a possible presidential candidate. A supporter commissioned English émigré, William G. Browne, Jr. to travel to Walnut Springs, near Monterey. Browne painted Taylor in a military setting so that people could see his accomplishments.
Painted by William Garl Browne Jr., 1847 / National Portrait Gallery, Smithsonian Institution NPG.71.57

Peggy never wanted to be First Lady. She wanted to stay in their log cabin in Louisiana where they had finally settled after the war, which had a rose garden and a view of the Mississippi River. Peggy only wanted to live peacefully with her husband by her side.

But Americans had another idea. And Peggy was always the dutiful wife. As President Zachary had said, she was a soldier in her own right. But by the time Margaret had made it to the White House, she was sick and tired. By then, three of her six children had died. She gave the official White House hostess job to her daughter Elizabeth "Betty" Bliss who was charming. President Taylor understood, but the public made up stories about the First Lady.

Because the public rarely saw her, people thought Peggy was locked up in the attic. They made up a rumor that she smoked a pipe made of corncob. They said that because she was brought up on a tobacco plantation. The truth was that she knew how to behave in society life. Her father was a wealthy tobacco plantation owner and a veteran of the American Revolution, and Peggy grew up playing with Nellie Custis, Martha Washington's granddaughter.

Peggy was private because she made that promise to stay away from society life. She only left the White House to go to daily church services at nearby St. John's Episcopal Church on Lafayette Square, and she visited with family and friends in her room at the Executive Mansion.

Dutiful First Lady

Guests said that Peggy always spoke about her husband's policies. She supported him on the frontier and now as First Lady. Peggy listened to her husband's ideas and debated issues. That's how she stayed involved, even though her body was failing her. She didn't like to be the center of attention and would never want anything written about her. Only one picture was ever found of her.

Then one day, President Zachary Taylor attended the groundbreaking ceremony at the Washington Monument on the hot morning of July 4, 1850. He strolled along the Potomac, drank a lot of water, and later ate a bowl of cherries and gulped down a glass of milk. That night in the Executive Mansion, his stomach began to ache. He endured great pain for five days. He died five days later from a condition known as "cholera morbus." It was caused by bacteria in food and water. How could he survive 40 years of military service and then die from bad food?

That is why on the morning of his funeral on July 13, 1850, Margaret Taylor was sobbing and shaking and could not get out of her bed. After sacrificing so much as an army wife, she was not prepared for this cruel turn of fate.

Approximately 100,000 people watched the presidential hearse proceed down the streets of Washington D.C. President Taylor's horse, Old Whitey, stood behind his coffin with boots turned backwards in his military saddle. What a sad day for the country.

Peggy's heart was broken. President Millard Fillmore, the next president, said Peggy could stay for a while in the Executive Mansion, but Peggy left that evening and she never mentioned the place again.

Death of Zachary Taylor
12th President of the United States
at the Presidents House, July 9th, 1850, 35 minutes past 10:00 P.M.

In this hand-colored lithograph on paper (1850) by Nathaniel Currier, Mrs. Taylor is portrayed in black.

National Portrait Gallery, Smithsonian Institution NPG.82.15

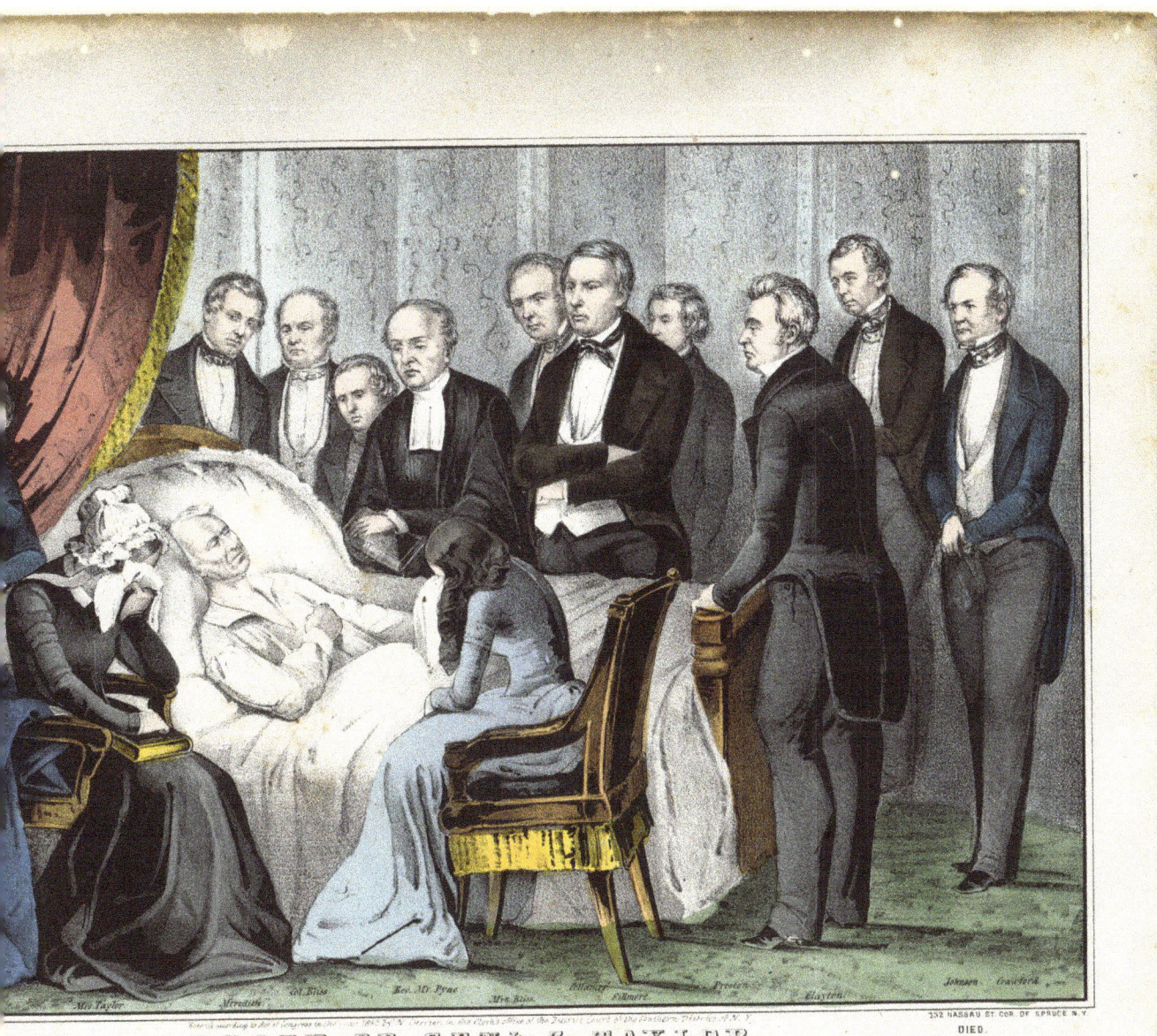

Because of her vow of privacy, there is only one photographic image of Margaret Taylor.

Because of Peggy's delicate condition, her daughter Elizabeth "Betty" Bliss assumed the role as White House hostess.

Guests said that Peggy always spoke about her husband's policies.

MARGARET MACKALL SMITH TAYLOR
First Lady to 12th President (1849 – 1850)

Margaret ("Peggy") Mackall Smith Taylor was born on September 21, 1788. The youngest daughter of seven children (three brothers and three sisters), her father was a wealthy tobacco plantation owner in Maryland and also a major in the Continental Army during the American Revolution. Her mother was Ann Hance Mackall. Peggy was most likely raised like other daughters of plantation owners. That education included sewing, embroidery, music, dancing, and managing servants.

Peggy had five daughters and one son: Anne Mackall, Sarah Knox, Octavia Pannell, Margaret Smith, Mary Elizabeth "Betty," and Richard "Dick" Scott. By the time she was 32, Peggy had already lost two of her daughters to a fever in the same year, 1820. Octavia was three, and Margaret was one. Fifteen years later, Sarah, who was married to Jefferson Davis, the president of the Confederate states that seceded from the Union during the Civil War, died three months after she was married in Bayou Sara, Louisiana, which was coincidentally in the same place as Octavia Pannell and Margaret Smith.

Anne attended school at a female academy in Kentucky; Sarah in Kentucky and Ohio; Betty in Pennsylvania; and Dick graduated from Yale University.

She was an army wife while her husband Zachary fought in the War of 1812, the Black Hawk War, the Seminole War, and the Mexican War which took place between 1846 and 1848.

Peggy was deeply heartbroken over the loss of her daughter Sarah from malaria. To help her grief, Peggy taught other military wives to grow vegetables, and make fresh butter and milk at the Baton Rouge Cottage.

During the Mexican War, Peggy stayed behind and prayed. She made a private chapel in their home. She encouraged local people, and the Episcopalian Church of St. James was formed. She was by Zachary's side at a parade honoring him as a hero of the Mexican War.

Although Peggy attended no public functions, as first lady she ordered meals, supervised the gardens, kitchen, and the servants. Peggy also took care of her husband's health and advised him about his wardrobe.

After President Taylor's death, Peggy lived a comfortable life as a widow. She attended the wedding of her son Richard, a general of the Confederate Army, to Louise Myrthe Bringier, a wealthy heiress. Some say she taught Sunday School.

Of English and Scottish descent, she was medium height with brown hair and brown eyes, and in 2010, a picture of her was finally found.

Peggy died suddenly while visiting with her daughter Betty in Pascagoula, Mississippi on August 14, 1852 at the age of 63. Peggy is buried with her husband at the Zachary Taylor National Cemetery in Louisville, Kentucky.

Monument to Zachary Taylor, the 12th President of the United States, and the mausoleum which houses his remains and his wife Margaret's at the Zachary Taylor National Cemetery in Louisville, Kentucky.
Library of Congress highsm.63898

Courtesy of Cooper Hewitt, Smithsonian Design Museum 1948-2-2

VISIT:

**Zachary Taylor National Cemetery
Jefferson County, Kentucky**

The cemetery was established in 1928 by an act of Congress initiated by the Taylor family to have the government take title to the family burial site where President Zachary Taylor was interred.

A mausoleum houses the remains of Zachary Taylor and his wife, Margaret.

Mid-19th Century Textile

This textile in colors of various browns, red and bright blue shows General Zachary Taylor at the battle of Palo Alto during the Mexican War. The scene has a wreath of roses, rosebuds and other flowers, too. It was done on cotton with a technique called block and roller. It was printed on plain weave.

ABIGAIL POWERS FILLMORE

The White House Guest List That Spoke Volumes

Abigail Powers Fillmore grew up poor but had thousands of books she inherited when her father, a Baptist minister, died when she was only two. Taught by her mother and her older brother, she became a teacher. She taught and studied with her student, a poor farm boy named Millard who was two years younger than her. They fell in love with books and each other. He always carried a dictionary and read all the time to work his way out of poverty. Millard became a lawyer, Abigail's husband and eventually the 13th President of the United States.

President Fillmore knew how much Abigail loved books. When they moved into the White House upon the sudden death of President Zachary Taylor, he made sure his wife would have a library. Congress gave them $2,000 to purchase history books, geography books, and the classics and then an extra $250 for Abigail to fill those shelves with works by Charles Dickens, William Makepeace Thackeray, and Washington Irving.

Abigail Powers Fillmore established the first White House Library.

The First Library

This turned the oval parlor room into the White House's first library in 1852. Prior to that, presidents would bring their own books and take them home, never even leaving a dictionary or a Bible.

Now there was a mahogany bookcase that Abigail selected herself. Great literary works lined the shelves behind the glass enclosure and included Shakespeare's plays, Robert Burns's poetry, Benjamin Franklin's autobiography, and other works by the founding fathers. Abigail also had many books of geography filled with maps that opened up the world to readers. There was a dictionary for learning new words and a Bible for strengthening faith.

Inspired by her new role and room, Abigail started sending the invitations to authors. She even invited her favorite author, William Makepeace Thackeray. The bookish teacher Abigail couldn't wait to meet him! Thackeray, the journalist turned novelist who wrote "Vanity Fair," was coming all the way from England.

To prepare for the evening, the White House staff rushed around to dust the room's piano, harp, and bookcase. On the newly installed kitchen stove that President Millard Fillmore and Abigail added, water boiled to be poured into Abigail's treasured pink and white china teapot. As the desserts were set out, Abigail dressed for the evening in a gown sewn by a machine. Stunningly beautiful, she was less about fashion and more about intellectual pursuits.

Abigail Fillmore was the first First Lady to wear a dress not sewn by hand.

Even though she had a bad ankle and couldn't stand for long hours, entertaining authors and even opera singers were more to Abigail's liking. On Friday evenings, the first lady gave the task of greeting hundreds and hundreds of White House guests on long receiving lines for hours and hours to her daughter. Mary "Abby" Abigail was beautiful, highly educated, and musically talented. Standing and small chat was not Abigail Fillmore's thing. She would much rather read. But she would never miss an opportunity to talk to her beloved writers in the library.

Before she was first lady, Abigail Fillmore had met Charles Dickens at the White House on March 13, 1842. The literary superstar was on his American Tour with Ebenezeer Scrooge still floating around in his imagination. Abigail was there with Millard, then a New York congressman. Dickens was famous for his novels such as the "Pickwick Papers," "Oliver Twist" and "Nicholas Nickelby."

In 1853, Abigail sent out an invitation to another one of her favorite authors, Washington Irving. President Fillmore had met Irving at Mount Vernon, the home of George Washington. Irving was researching a biography he was writing about the first president. By that time, the beloved Irving had already published stories about a "pipe smoking and wagon riding" Saint Nicholas. He also gave the world Rip Van Winkle who slept through the American Revolution, as well as the Legend of Sleepy Hollow, a mysterious tale about a lanky schoolteacher named Ichabod Crane who disappeared in the woods.

In that parlor room, Abigail and her guests had a chance to chat with Washington Irving and enjoy a cup of tea. Perhaps they even asked what really happened to Ichabod Crane. Did he go missing because of the Headless Horseman?

After all was said and done, Abigail Fillmore would retire to her bedroom to rest. She covered herself with the tumbling-block quilt she sewed herself and read by candlelight.

Painting of Abigail Fillmore
The gold chain that hangs from her neck in this portrait would have been attached to a watch to be used to keep up with her busy social schedule. c. 1840
National Portrait Gallery, Smithsonian Institution S/NPG.78.20

Before she was First Lady, Abigail Fillmore had met Charles Dickens at the White House on March 13, 1842.

Abigail Fillmore sewed this quilt.
The pattern is called Tumbling Block.
Still in excellent condition, it is on her bed at the historic
Millard Fillmore House in East Aurora, New York.

Used with permission of Aurora Historical Society, East Aurora, New York

Abigail Fillmore
Library of Congress cph.3a05526

**Some Books
On The Shelves
of the First
White House Library:**

Aesop's Fables

Arabian Nights

Bible

The Works of Francis Bacon

The Works of Robert Burns

Encyclopedia Americana

The Works of
Benjamin Franklin

The Works of
Washington Irving

Thomas Jefferson Memoir

The Works of Samuel Johnson

The Writings of
George Washington

Webster's Dictionary

ABIGAIL POWERS FILLMORE
First Lady to 13th President (1850 – 1853)

Abigail Powers Fillmore was born on March 13, 1798 in Stillwater, New York. After her father, the Reverend Lemuel Leland Powers, died, her mother Abigail Newland Powers moved all seven children to Moravia, New York. Abigail was the youngest, and her family was poor.

Educated by her mother and brother with her father's books, Abigail loved literature and excelled at math, history, government, philosophy, and geography. She became a teacher herself.

At New Hope Academy in New York, Abigail and her student Millard Fillmore, two years her junior, fell in love. Tall and handsome, Millard was an apprentice at a cloth mill and would spend his days teaching himself new words from a dictionary.

The couple courted for seven years, and three of those years were long distance as Millard studied to be a lawyer. They married on February 5, 1826 in a small ceremony with no honeymoon. They had two children, a son Millard Powers and a daughter Mary "Abby" Abigail.

The couple established a lending library and a college in Buffalo, New York.

In 1850, Abigail Fillmore unexpectedly became the First Lady. President Zachary Taylor was in office only 16 months when he shockingly died after a brief illness. Millard Fillmore, his vice president, became the "accidental" president. Now this couple who began their life in poverty found themselves living in the White House.

Abigail was the first First Lady to grow up in poverty, the first to work before getting married, and the first to work outside of the home. At a time when many women did not get a formal education, Abigail's love of books encouraged future generations of women to go to school. Her life also encouraged many women to become teachers.

In addition, Abigail played piano, gardened, and sewed. She loved to go to museums, art galleries, theater, concerts and lectures, and also loved to go "sea bathing" which was soaking in the sea to improve health.

She is credited with creating the first White House Library. A prominent politician and attorney Daniel Webster had a personal assistant, Charles Lanman, who helped select the original books with the appropriations from Congress.

Abigail Fillmore attended the inauguration of President Franklin Pierce on March 4, 1853, which was a freezing and windy day. She caught a cold which progressed into pneumonia. She died at the age of 55 at the Willard Hotel in Washington D.C. on March 30, 1853, only 26 days after leaving the White House.

Millard Fillmore remarried Caroline Carmichael McIntosh, a wealthy widow from Buffalo, New York, five years later.

Abigail's tumbling-block quilt is still on the bed for visitors to see at the Millard Fillmore House, a historic house museum, built in 1826, in East Aurora, New York. She is buried with her husband and their two children, and also Millard's second wife, Caroline Carmichael McIntosh Fillmore.

Inside the Fillmore home, you can find Abigail's mahogany bookcase filled with books. It is not in the White House because Franklin Delano Roosevelt established the current White House library.

In keeping with family tradition, Abigail's nephew Dr. Cyrus Powers founded the historic Powers Library in Moravia, New York.

VISIT:

**Millard Fillmore House
24 Shearer Avenue
East Aurora, NY 14052**

an historic house museum

aurorahistoricalsociety.com

Abigail Fillmore Portrait
Used with permission of Aurora Historical Society, East Aurora, New York

ELIZA McCARDLE JOHNSON

Courtesy of the Andrew Johnson National Historic Site

The First Children's Party at the Executive Mansion

In the winter of 1868, a young lady named Fanny Gedney was one of 300 children to receive this invitation:

Juvenile Soiree
given by the
Children of the President's Family
at the Executive Mansion
Tuesday evening December 29, 1868

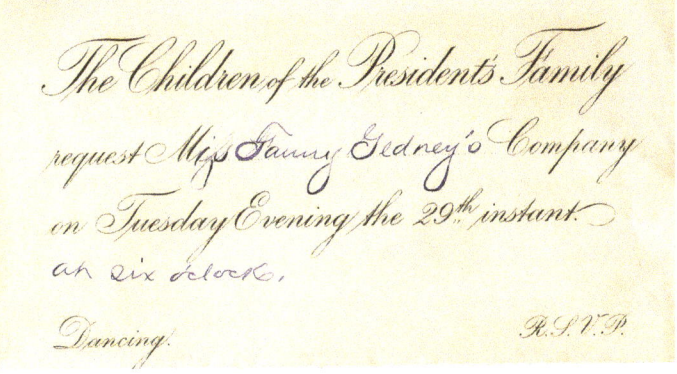

The response card said the party would begin at 6:00 p.m. There would be dancing conducted under the direction of Messrs. L.G. Marini and H. Bates. The occasion was to celebrate the 60th birthday of President Andrew Johnson.

This was the first ever children's party held in the Executive Mansion, now called the White House.

This was also one of the few parties that First Lady Eliza Johnson attended. She was not a physically well woman. After the birth of Eliza's fifth child and the accidental death of her son Charles, Eliza's health took a turn for the worse. She had tuberculosis, which back then was treated by remaining indoors. Eliza rarely left her reclining chair in her room on the second floor of the Executive Mansion.

The only child of a poor shoemaker and a quiltmaker, Eliza made sandals and quilts. She wore simple clothing in expensive fabric. She loved to do embroidery and read poetry. She also read the newspapers at the local and national level, clipping the articles about her husband President Andrew Johnson and saving them in a scrapbook. If they were good articles, she read them to him at night. If they were bad, she read them to him in the morning, not to disrupt his sleep.

Because of her ill health, Eliza had given the official White House hostess duty to her eldest daughter Martha Johnson Patterson who was married to a senator.

But on the night of December 29, 1868, Eliza was at the party seated in an armchair. Next to her was President Johnson and also their daughter and son-in-law, Martha and David Patterson, their widowed daughter Mary Stover, and sons Robert and Andrew, Jr.

Fanny Gedney, one of the 300 children who attended the Juvenile Soiree, and her invitation.

Courtesy of the Andrew Johnson National Historic Site

Fanny Gedney's Dance Card

One of Eliza's many clippings and scrapbooks

As promised, the party began promptly at 6:00 p.m., and President Johnson and the First Lady greeted the young guests. The five Johnson grandchildren were the real hosts: Lily Stover, 13; Sarah Drake Stover, 11; Andrew Johnson Patterson, 11; Belle Patterson, 9; and Andrew Johnson Stover, 8.

The young guests received dance cards, which contained the different types of dances and the composers of the songs.

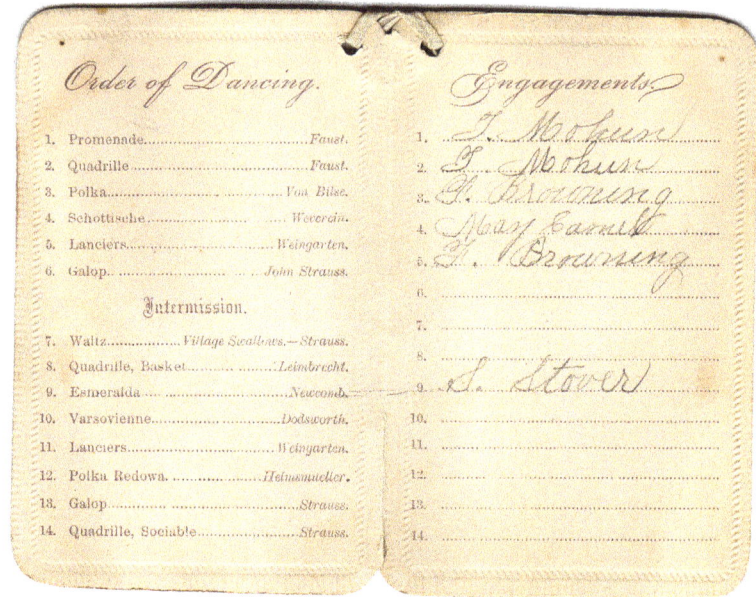

Below is the list of dances and composers:

1. Promenade...Faust
2. Quadrille..Faust
3. Polka...Von Bilse
4. Schottische..Wererein
5. Lanciers..Weingarten
6. Galop..John Strauss

INTERMISSION

7. Waltz..Village Swallows--Strauss
8. Quadrille, Basket...Leimbrecht
9. Esmeralda...Newcomb
10. Varsovienne..Dodsworth
11. Lanciers..Weingarten
12. Polka Redowa..Helmsmuller
13. Galop..Strauss
14. Quadrille, Sociable.. Strauss

Images Courtesy of the Andrew Johnson National Historic Site

Under the brightly lit chandeliers, students from a dance school helped the children learn the dances. The steps were quite involved. Then they all had cake and ice cream.

Not only did Eliza help children host the first party at the White House, but also a few months later in the spring, Eliza attended the Easter Egg Roll, which was moved from the U.S. Capitol to the White House. Afternoons prior to that Easter Monday, the Johnson children and grandchildren were dyeing eggs in the kitchen. That Monday, Eliza sat in her portico, which is another word for porch. Its roof sheltered her from the wind, and she was still close enough to have her heart sing with the laughter of children. She could see the smiles on their faces as they rolled the colorful eggs down the great lawn. The Easter Egg Roll has been held at the White House ever since.

Eliza began her role as first lady unexpectedly after the assassination of President Abraham Lincoln. The Civil War ended, the slaves were emancipated, and her husband was asked to step into the shoes of one of the most wonderful leaders this world has ever known. Not a public person, Eliza would have been quite content to enjoy her private life back home in Tennessee with her family. History had another plan for her.

First Lady Eliza Johnson was always a kind and peaceful presence for her large family. She was a rock, in spirit and mind, for her husband, especially during his impeachment proceedings. It is no wonder President Johnson and their children and grandchildren adored her.

Eliza Johnson spent much time in her "invalid's chair" upstairs in her room at the White House. It is now at the Johnson National Historic Site.

Courtesy of the Andrew Johnson National Historic Site

Eliza Johnson
Images Courtesy of the Andrew Johnson National Historic Site

Eliza's sewing needles

sewing bird

embroidery

ELIZA McCARDLE JOHNSON
First Lady to 17th President (1865 – 1869)

Eliza McCardle Johnson was born on October 4, 1810 in Leesburg, Tennessee. She was the only child of John McCardle, a poor shoemaker, and Sarah Phillips, a quilter. Eliza quit school after the 8th grade to help earn money by quilting.

She is the youngest first lady to be married. As the story goes, Eliza spotted Andrew riding horseback into Greeneville, Tennessee from North Carolina to establish a tailor shop. They married soon thereafter on May 17, 1827. She was only 17.

Credited with helping him rise from poverty into politics, Eliza taught Andrew Johnson how to write, do arithmetic, and encouraged him to join the Greenville Debating Society. This helped him become a good public speaker, something which attracted Abraham Lincoln who asked him to be his vice president. Eliza had been educated at The Rhea Academy in a log cabin. Andrew never attended school. The couple had five children: Martha, Charles, Mary, Robert, and Andrew, Jr.

In her younger days, Eliza kept house by cooking and cleaning, growing her own vegetables, and making clothes. She played an active role in the education of her children. She was a good money manager and saved enough to buy bigger homes and rental properties. She was a Methodist who opposed slavery.

When President Lincoln sent Andrew Johnson to Nashville during the Civil War in 1862, Eliza stayed home with the family. The Confederates burned down their house, and Eliza and her children were homeless. They were wartime refugees, and this created much anxiety for her. The family finally rejoined Andrew in Nashville months later. By 1865 Eliza had lost a son in the war and a son-in-law. She became ill with tuberculosis after the birth of her fifth child. The stress of homelessness and the death of her son Charles worsened her condition. She would remain frail for the rest of her life.

That's why it took her a few months to gain her strength to join her husband in the White House and leave their home in Tennessee. Eliza used a congressional appropriation of $30,000 to refurbish the Executive Mansion. Thanks to her, two cows lived on its lawn to provide fresh milk.

Abraham Lincoln was a Republican, and Andrew Johnson was a Democrat. After Lincoln was assassinated on April 15, 1865, Johnson was sworn in as president.

Andrew Johnson was the first president to be impeached for "high crimes and misdemeanors," but Eliza always took his side. She was his biggest supporter. It could be said that he was a most unpopular president, but popular with his family. When he escaped conviction in the Senate by one vote, Eliza exclaimed, "I knew he'd be acquitted; I knew it."

Their son Robert died from an accidental overdose eight weeks after his father's presidential term ended. Eliza died, six months after her husband, at the age of 65 on January 15, 1876 in her daughter Martha Johnson Patterson's Tennessee home. Martha, the consummate hostess, said about her mother, "She was the stepping stone to all the honors and fame my father attained."

Eliza is buried alongside her husband at the Andrew Johnson National Cemetery in Greeneville, Tennessee.

VISIT:
The Andrew Johnson National Historic Site
101 N College Street, in Greeneville, Tennessee 37743
nps.gov/anjo

Counterclockwise:

Eliza's French candy box; her sewing machine; her bedroom with her golden oak furniture in the Andrew Johnson Homestead, Andrew Johnson National Historic Site. According to family tradition, she made the quilt.

Images Courtesy of the Andrew Johnson National Historic Site

FRANCES CLARA FOLSOM CLEVELAND

Courtesy of the National Portrait Gallery, Smithsonian Institution NPG.2007.292

The 19th Century's "It Girl"

Frances Cleveland was an "influencer." At 21, she took the country by storm when news broke that she was to marry President Grover Cleveland, aged 49, in the White House.

Who was this young lady who had stolen the heart of the President? The country was fascinated. And on the couple's wedding day, the media couldn't wait to get a glimpse of her.

On the morning of June 2, 1886, the presidential carriage waited for Frances, her mother Emma, and her cousin Benjamin to arrive by train. They had stayed in New York City since Decoration Day, which is now called Memorial Day.

Rose Cleveland, the sister of President Grover Cleveland, greeted Frances and her family. The newspapermen got off that train and swarmed them like paparazzi. The coachman, Hawkins, cracked his whip, and the horses galloped to the White House, doing their best to get away from the sketch artists and reporters.

Secret Romance

Grover Cleveland was the most eligible bachelor of that time. He had served as mayor of Buffalo, New York and governor of New York. He once joked that he was waiting for his bride to grow up. And that's what he did.

Grover Cleveland was a bachelor when he took office on March 4, 1885. Until his marriage, Grover's sister Rose Cleveland, called the "lady of the land," was the hostess.

When Grover Cleveland began his career as a lawyer in Buffalo, his partner was Oscar Folsom, Frances's father. When Frances was a little girl, they called her Frank. Grover bought her a baby carriage and became known as "Uncle Cleve." Days after Frank turned 11, her father died in a carriage accident. Since her father died without a will, the court named Grover as administrator of the estate. Grover looked after Frank and her mother who moved to live with relatives before both settling back in Buffalo.

Grover supervised their finances and made sure Frank earned a college education. When she studied at Wells College, he sent her letters and flowers. She began calling herself Frances and left the nickname behind. The huge age difference didn't matter to them. They dated in secret and were engaged for two years.

Grover was a plain, simple, and stout man. When he wasn't working (which was unusual), Grover loved to go fishing and shoot squirrels. He believed a woman's place was in the home and with family. Newspaper reporters watched the president's every move, and that always bothered him.

Frances charmed anyone who had the good fortune to meet her, near and far. The famous author Mark Twain called her "the young, the beautiful, the good-hearted, the sympathetic, the fascinating." To prepare her for the role as first lady, the White House sent Frances and her mother to Europe. They visited seven European countries during nine months. Frances learned about social customs and historic sites. In France, she prepared her trousseau – the items a bride needs such as garments and linens.

While waiting for his bride to arrive on their wedding day, President Cleveland was working and only took about two or three breaks to chat with Frances and her mother. He even went for a drive in the afternoon.

Just before 7:00 p.m., the famous conductor John Phillip Sousa raised his baton and the Marine Band played Mendelsohn's "Wedding March." The couple walked slowly down the stairs. President Cleveland wore a black suit. On his arm, Frances looked like a princess and stunned in a cream satin

Cleveland was the first Democrat to win the presidency in 25 years. The Democrats were thrilled. On his wedding day, the country came together to celebrate his choice for a wife.

Photograph of Frances Cleveland

by Frances Benjamin Johnston, c.1897

Courtesy of the National Portrait Gallery, Smithsonian Institution S/NPG.77.57

wedding gown, trimmed in orange blossoms and leaves. The 15-foot-train filled the length of the Blue Room.

A guest later described Frances as a "radiant vision of young springtime." She loved flowers, and they surrounded her from the greenhouse. Reporters were not permitted to attend the ceremony. Detailed accounts came from the approximately 30 wedding guests, which included a few family members and Cabinet officers. Under the magnificent chandelier, The Reverend Dr. Byron Sunderland of the First Presbyterian Church performed the ceremony which lasted about 10 minutes. He was assisted by Grover's younger brother, The Reverend William Cleveland.

Afterwards, the group moved to the East Parlor, decorated with rare palms and foliage. Then they ate in the dining room filled with potted plants, arranged pyramid style in the corners of the room, along with roses on the mirrors.

Grover gave Frances a diamond necklace. The couple gave their guests satin boxes from Tiffany's with their signature on small cards on the lids, and inside each was a piece of cake. (Some of the boxes still survive!) A 21-gun salute celebrated the wedding, and all church bells rang throughout the land.

At 8:30 p.m., President and First Lady Cleveland made their getaway. They left through a private exit in the Blue Room and traveled by carriage to the railway. They boarded a special train to Deer Park, Maryland, 200 miles away, for a short honeymoon in a cottage in the Allegheny Mountains.

Of course, the reporters followed. The newspapermen and the sketch artists waited in the treetops and around the properties to capture an image of the couple, especially Frances who charmed and fascinated the hearts and minds of Americans.

From that point on, Frances was not left alone. The image of the First Lady went "viral" in newspapers and ads. It was Frank-mania!

Enchanting, fashionable, and kind, Frances had a lovely voice and a smile that never appeared the same way twice. Men adored her, and women wanted to be like her. Even President Cleveland became a better dresser and better with social graces. Women copied her hairstyles and fashion sense, and manufacturers wanted her to endorse their products.

Piano makers called to send pianos to the White House. Frances also received sewing machines, fabrics, and perfumes. Her picture was used as a product endorsement because she had the magic touch. The image of Frances Cleveland appeared on plates, jewelry, picture cards, textiles, and glassware, and without her approval. Her image was used to sell so many things including needles and thread, headache remedies, and beauty products. For many magazines, she was their cover girl.

President and First Lady Cleveland finished out the term in 1889. When President Harrison took office, Frances promised they'd be back, and she was right. President Cleveland was re-elected in 1893. In the meantime, their daughter Ruth was born. Frances Cleveland, the only first lady to serve two non-consecutive terms, also achieved another first. Baby Esther, her second daughter of five children, was the first and only child born in the White House.

President Grover Cleveland married Miss Frances Folsom at the White House on June 2, 1886 in the Blue Room.

From an engraving in Frank Leslie's *Illustrated Weekly,* New York, June 12, 1886 / *Library of Congress cph.3a07967*

FRANCES CLARA FOLSOM CLEVELAND
First Lady to 22nd and 24th President (1886 – 1889 and 1893 –1897)

Frances Cleveland
Courtesy of the National Portrait Gallery, Smithsonian Institution
NPG.2007.292

Library of Congress pga.01868

According to the Curtiss Candy Company, the Baby Ruth Candy Bar was named after Ruth Cleveland, Frances and Grover's daughter.

Frances Clara Folsom Cleveland was born on July 21, 1864 in Buffalo, New York to parents Oscar Folsom and Emma Harmon. They lived at 168 Edward Street, and the house still remains and is marked with a sign, though it is not considered a National Historic Landmark. Her sister Nellie Augusta died shortly after her first birthday in 1872. Frances grew up an only child.

Her father Oscar Folsom, a wealthy lawyer, died on July 23, 1875 in a carriage accident. Her mother Emma Harmon Folsom Perrine remarried, 16 years after the death of her husband, to Edward Perrine. Her grandfather Colonel John B. Folsom, whom she adored, had died 16 days before the wedding.

She and President Grover Cleveland had five children: Ruth, Esther, Marion, Richard, and Francis Grover. Ruth died on January 7, 1904 at the age of 12 from diphtheria. According to the Curtiss Candy Company, the Baby Ruth candy bar was later named after her. Esther was the first baby born in the White House during Cleveland's second term.

Frances attended the Medina Academy and Buffalo's Central High School. She enrolled at Wells College in Aurora, New York, which was one of the first liberal arts colleges for women.

Frances did not champion a woman's right to vote, nor did her husband. At one point she was the second vice president for the New Jersey Association of the Anti-Suffrage Movement from 1913 until 1920 when women won the right to vote. Although she voted, she did not feel it was necessary.

Because of her popularity and to keep some privacy for her children, she closed the White House grounds to the public.

Whenever Frances felt compelled to get involved with a political issue, President Cleveland insisted that she pay attention to home and family.

Frances held informal receptions on Saturday mornings for working women and shop girls who had to work during the week. She wanted them be able to visit the White House.

Frances worked to promote free kindergartens in Washington D.C. and New York City.

She held an Authors' Reception at the White House, attended by Mark Twain among others, to bring attention to the need for laws to protect people from having their image used on products without permission. President Cleveland tried, but met with opposition.

National Portrait Gallery, Smithsonian Institution; gift of John O'Brien NPG.91.114

Mrs. Thomas J. Preston, Jr. (formerly Mrs. Grover Cleveland) served as President of The Needlework Guild of America for the seventh time and entered her work at the Guild's 50th Convention in Philadelphia in 1933.

VISIT:

**Grover Cleveland Birthplace Historic Site
207 Bloomfield Ave.
Caldwell, NJ 07006**

Personal artifacts of former President Cleveland and Frances, including a piece of wedding cake in a box.

presidentcleveland.org

**The Buffalo History
1 Museum Ct.
Buffalo, NY 14216**

This museum resides in the sole-surviving permanent structure from the New York State pavilion for the Pan-American Exposition in 1901.

buffalohistory.org

During the second term, Frances was the first presidential wife to pay a call on a head of state, Queen Regent of Spain.

During World War I and the Great Depression, Frances became involved with the Needlework Guild and eventually served as president. The organization donated clothing to the needy around the world.

Grover had suffered from mouth cancer and was secretly operated on in a yacht. After dealing with poor health, he died from a heart attack in his home in 1908. Frances married an archaeology professor from Princeton University named Thomas Jex Preston, Jr., five years later, on February 10, 1913 in a private ceremony hosted by First Lady Helen Taft. Frances was the first First Lady to marry after widowhood. Jacqueline Kennedy Onassis was the next.

In 1911, philanthropist Andrew Carnegie endowed Wells College's library, and it was named in her honor. Frances used her fame to inspire young women and remained active with her alma mater where she served on its Board of Trustees for 40 years.

She made her last public appearance at its June 1946 bicentennial celebration, along with President and First Lady Truman, Edith Wilson, Herbert Hoover, and General Dwight D. Eisenhower.

Frances was instrumental in founding Douglass College, a women's college, now part of Rutgers University.

She had cataract surgery to restore her sight, but learned braille to read beforehand.

Frances died in her sleep on October 29, 1947 at the age of 83 in Baltimore, Maryland. She is buried in Princeton Cemetery in New Jersey next to her husband Grover and Baby Ruth.

Kind, thoughtful, and caring, Frances was known to shake 6,000 hands in one day. Although she kept her place in the home and with family and stayed out of politics, Frances elevated the role of the first lady to a public figure.

Her wedding gown is preserved at the Smithsonian Institution.

On the 150th anniversary of her birthday, there was a ceremony at the Robert H. Jackson United States Courthouse in Buffalo, New York.

Frances Cleveland appeared on the cover of magazines, as well as on many items without her permission. There are probably more items with Frances Cleveland's likeness than any other first lady. Her image appeared on beauty products, plates, playing cards, cigar boxes, needles and thread, and many other things.

From the Mark D. Evans Collection, Avon, NY

IDA SAXTON MCKINLEY

Counting Stitches, Cozy Slippers

Ida was called the schoolgirl of the Civil War. She helped her mother sew uniforms for soldiers. And she was good at counting stitches.

Ida also counted stitches in needlepoint and crochet with her grandmother in their Ohio home.

In school, Ida was good in math. She could count in French, Latin and Greek, too! She counted music notes, beats with her feet, and miles on long hikes.

After graduation, Ida toured Europe. In Belgium, she watched old women braid crochet threads into the finest lace. They worked hard for many hours and little pay. Ida bought lots of lace from them.

There Ida also met Charles Felu, an artist who painted with his feet. He was born with no arms. She would never forget him. Ida came home and worked with her father at a bank. She was good at counting money, too.

Ida and Major

Major William "Bill" McKinley walked in the bank one day. He was a Civil War veteran and a lawyer. She liked to call him "Major." He told Ida he had fallen in love when he first spotted her eating a creamed chicken waffle at a picnic!

Bill fell in love with Ida when she was eating a chicken waffle! Before the Civil War, chicken and waffles were fancy breakfast meals at plantation homes.

Ida married Bill in church in front of 1,000 people. Then Bill McKinley ran for Congress and won. Ida said, "One day, you'll be President of the United States!"

They had two daughters who died young. Ida's mother died, too. Ida became sick with sadness and suffered from seizures. Bill cared for her.

To pass the time, Ida crocheted in her rocking chair. She kept a picture of Bill in her silk bag of yarn.

She remembered her mother sewing uniforms; she remembered old women making lace; and she remembered the artist painting with his feet.

When Ida crocheted, she felt better.

One day, Ida made a pair of blue slippers. She counted seven rows, stitched wool tops, and tied a satin ribbon bow. She sewed leather soles and signed her name.

Then she made a pair in ivory. Another in grey. Another in purple. But she never made a pair in yellow.

She made 50 slippers, 100 slippers, 200 slippers!

She had too many slippers…

So she gave them away!

To a friend. To a neighbor. To a stranger.

To veterans. To orphans. To hospital patients.

And every time she gave, everyone felt better. Ida did too.

Major had also been busy. He did become the 25th President of the United States. Now, Ida was First Lady!

When the White House received requests, Ida donated slippers to auctions. They were raffled off to help charities.

Even though she was frail, Ida was never too sick or too tired to make another pair of slippers. She rode in an open carriage. The coachman carried slippers into hospitals, orphanages, homeless shelters and old age homes. She was their princess. Everyone wanted Ida's slippers.

When the 19th President of the United States Rutherford B. Hayes had become ill, Ida sent him a pair, too. She later sent slippers to President Theodore Roosevelt's son, Archie.

Ida gave away 4,000 pairs of slippers. Many are in museums today. And on the bottom of the soles, you can still read her signature – Made by Mrs. Wm. McKinley.

Ida's blue crocheted slippers
Courtesy of the First Ladies' Library

Crocheting was Ida's way of helping others the best she could.

Ida crocheted and donated approximately 4,000 pairs of slippers.

The color blue was her signature color.

The word crochet comes from "croc," or "croche," which is the Middle French word for "hook."

The Old Norse word for "hook" is "krokr."

IDA SAXTON MCKINLEY
First Lady to 25th President (1897 – 1901)

Ida was born on June 8, 1847 in Canton, Ohio into a life of wealth and privilege to parents James Asbury Saxton and Kate (DeWalt) Saxton who was well-educated for a woman of that era. James Asbury Saxton, president of Stark Bank, had also owned a hardware store, developed real estate and owned property. Ida had a younger sister Mary (Pina) and a younger brother George.

She attended the best boarding and finishing schools in Ohio, New York, and Pennsylvania. Principal Betsy Mix Cowles, an early leader in the Women's Movement, encouraged Ida's skills in mathematics, as did her father.

In 1869, Ida visited 10 European countries in six months. Beautiful and strong, Ida could walk 10 miles a day. She went horseback riding and fell in love with the poetry of Robert Burns. She bought Belgium lace which she wore the rest of her life. She also brought home a music box from Switzerland for her mother. Ida loved music, played piano, danced, sang, and excelled at playing cards.

Ida became a manager of Stark Bank in Canton, Ohio where her father served as the bank's president. It was unusual for a woman to work in a bank during those days.

Ida McKinley
The picture of her "Major,"
President Bill McKinley
is on the table.
Library of Congress cph.3c24997

Library of Congress cph.3b00464

She met and married "Major" William McKinley on January 25, 1871. Unfortunately, their two daughters, Katie and Little Ida died young.

She was the most formally educated first lady up until that time.

She was the first First Lady to invite musicians to entertain after state dinners. She was also the first person to appear in a photograph on the cover of "Ladies' Home Journal" in January 1898.

Ida loved roses and lilies of the valley. Roses have been named after her, and they are called The American Ida and the Mrs. McKinley. The roses are light pink with dark pink edges.

Ida had a condition known as epilepsy, and she had seizures.

Crocheting was her way of helping others the best she could. The color blue, her signature color, was soothing to her condition. Yellow was not.

President William McKinley was assassinated on September 6, 1901 in Buffalo, New York at the Pan-American Exposition (World's Fair) in the Temple of Music. Ida was by his side until he died on September 14, 1901. She went to live with her sister. She kept donating her crocheted slippers. Ida died on May 26, 1907.

In Canton, Ohio, Ida is buried with her husband and their two daughters at the McKinley Monument and Tomb.

The First Ladies' National Historic Site, managed by the First Ladies' Library, is housed in two buildings, and one is the Ida Saxton McKinley Historic Home at 205 Market Avenue South. It is open to the public. There you can see her piano, music box, tiara, and the crocheted slippers.

Ida Saxton McKinley, President William McKinley, and his mother, Nancy Allison McKinley

Their ancestral home is now the site of the First Ladies National Historic Site.

Also located in Canton! The William McKinley Presidential Library & Museum 800 McKinley Monument Drive NW

Courtesy of National Portrait Gallery, Smithsonian Institution NPG.91.86

VISIT:

The First Ladies National Historic Site in downtown Canton, Ohio.

Ancestral Home of First Lady Ida Saxton-McKinley
Museum/Saxton McKinley House
331 S. Market Avenue South
Canton, OH 44702

Education and Research Center
205 Market Avenue South
Canton, OH 44702

firstladies.org

Courtesy of the First Ladies' Library, located in Ida's ancestral home (left) in Ohio. The Education and Research Center (above).

EDITH KERMIT CAROW ROOSEVELT

Courtesy of the Sagamore Hill National Historic Site, National Park Service, Oyster Bay, NY

Mrs. Roosevelt's Renovations of the White House

Vice President Theodore Roosevelt was climbing Mount Tahawus when he received word that President William McKinley took a turn for the worse after being shot on September 6, 1901 at the Pan American Exposition in upstate New York. Roosevelt thought that McKinley was recovering from the two bullet wounds to his stomach, so he rejoined his family on vacation in this remote area of the Adirondacks.

Vice President Roosevelt made his way back, but when he arrived in Buffalo, New York, President McKinley had already died. It was September 14, 1901, and Roosevelt was sworn in as the 26th President of the United States.

President Theodore Roosevelt moved into the White House on September 23, 1901, and his family arrived two days later. That's when things really started to change.

Moving In

Like any mother does when moving into a new home, Edith checked out the rooms. She had to figure out where her large family would sleep. She was used to her home at Sagamore Hill in Oyster Bay, Long Island. It had 13 bedrooms for the children and guests and staff. To her surprise, her husband's office was located next to the living room on the second floor. How could they enjoy themselves with guests conducting business right next to them? She exclaimed to Theodore, "This is like living on top of a store!"

The other problem was the lack of space. No president ever had six children before. She took out her sketch book. Then she drew out plans to make the White House look like a comfortable home with a separate office for the president. She wanted it to look like the original 18th century Federalist style and be an historical showcase for the country, too.

Edith hired a prestigious architecture firm in New York by the name of McKim, Mead, and White. She also worked with her cousin, Edith Wharton, who wrote many novels, short stories and poems.

Impressed with Edith's plans, Congress approved the money needed to renovate the White House. Edith worked with the architects and the decorators. She was great with money and knew how to stay on a budget. She also had a keen sense of design. She approved all the house's fabrics, furniture, and paint colors.

Edith was good with money, excellent with decorating, and also very good at needlework.

Edith hired the White House's first Social Secretary, Isabelle Hagner, to help her keep track. And this is what she did.

The Office of the President (now the West Wing) was separated from the family living quarters on the second floor.

She rid the White House of its old-fashioned Victorian look. She threw away the velvet sofas, carpets, and lampshades with fringes. She redecorated the Green Room, Blue Room, and East Room with antiques, including the gorgeous Bohemian glass chandelier in the East Room.

When future presidents and first ladies would move out of the White House, they would take all of their paintings, furniture, and decorations. Edith would not have that anymore. What was in the White House was to stay in the White House. It belonged to the people.

Edith ordered fancy china for 120 people for their new dining room. Then it dawned on her. What happened to all of the other china? She spent years locating the plates and cups and saucers and

President Roosevelt officially named the Executive Mansion the "White House" in 1901.

found them from 25 previous administrations. That collection is now housed in the White House China Room.

She also didn't want the first ladies to be forgotten like the china. She realized that history had overlooked them. Edith collected their portraits and had the architects renovate the basement into a hallway where the portraits could be displayed for visitors to gaze into their faces, including hers. This became the First Ladies National Portrait Gallery.

Edith made the White House into a home for her family, an office for her husband, and a historical showcase for the country.

With her great sense of style and class, she revealed the new White House to the public at a reception on New Year's Day in 1903.

Edith Roosevelt cross-stitched this sampler of all the important moments in her husband's life.

Edith created the First Ladies Portrait Gallery so they would not be forgotten.

Courtesy of the Sagamore Hill National Historic Site, National Park Service, Oyster Bay, NY

EDITH KERMIT CAROW ROOSEVELT
First Lady to 26th President (1901 – 1909)

Edith Kermit Carow Roosevelt was born on August 6, 1861 in Norwich, Connecticut to Charles Carow, a shipping magnate and Gertrude Tyler Carow. She grew up in an old brownstone in New York's Union Square and attended Ms. Comstock's School.

She was a childhood friend of Theodore Roosevelt and his sister Corinne. Theodore even named his rowboat after her. Before he attended Harvard, they had a brief spat, and he married Alice Lee Hathaway who died after giving birth to their daughter Alice in 1884. His mother died on the same day, Valentine's Day. Theodore moved to the Badlands in the Dakotas to grieve, and when he visited his sister Corinne, he accidentally met Edith again.

Edith's family had moved to London because they had fallen upon hard times financially. The couple married secretly in London on December 2, 1886.

They had five children within a period of 10 years: Theodore, Jr., Kermit, Ethel, Archibald, and Quentin. They also had lots of pets. Quentin was shot down over German lines when he was 21. Edith suffered profound grief. Kermit became an alcoholic and committed suicide in 1943 while serving in the Army during World War II.

Theodore Roosevelt, Jr., the family's most decorated soldier, died a year later in 1944. A distinguished Army Officer, Archibald was wounded in both WWI and WWII, but he recovered and lived until 1979.

Edith took care of her husband who was a workaholic. Although the youngest president at 42 when he took office, he had heart disease. She purchased a retreat for them in a hunting shack, called Pine Knot, at the foothills of the Blue Ridge Mountains.

She preferred to be called Mrs. Roosevelt rather than First Lady. He did not like to be called Teddy. He preferred Colonel.

She loved music and White House entertainers included the Vienna Boys' Choir and the cellist Pablo Casals. The two social events of the White House years, however, were the wedding of "Princess Alice" to Nicholas Longworth, and Ethel's debutante "coming out" party.

Edith Roosevelt
A lifelong knitter, Edith was President of the local chapter of the Needlework Guild, a charity that provided garments for the poor through such organizations as the American Red Cross. She is seated here with one of her dogs.
Courtesy of the Sagamore Hill National Historic Site, National Park Service, Oyster Bay, NY

When this photograph was taken, the president's family was preparing to leave the White House and Roosevelt's successor, William Taft, was expected to become president. Edith is fourth from the left.
Courtesy of National Portrait Gallery, Smithsonian Institution, gift of Joanna Sturm
NPG.81.126

Her first love was reading. She was never seen without a book in her hand, especially Shakespeare. Her favorite plays were "MacBeth" and "As You Like It."

Theodore died in his sleep at the age of 60 on January 6, 1919 at Sagamore Hill. After he passed, Edith moved into the room once used by the Governess.

Edith lived 30 more years. She said that she had saltwater around her heart. She cruised to the Greek Isles, Caribbean, Latin America, Peru, Brazil, and Panama. She knew seven presidents personally. She campaigned against Franklin Delano Roosevelt ("FDR") in 1932. FDR was Theodore Roosevelt's 5th cousin.

Edith Roosevelt
Edith loved to read and was always seen with a book in her hand.

Photo by J. Schloss, NY, c 1902
Library of Congress, ppmsca.36316

This official citation recognizes Edith's work with the Needlework Guild of America, Inc.

Edith Roosevelt served as Secretary of the Board of The Little Sunbeam Sewing School. It existed from 1889 until 1916 and its mission was "the instruction of girls in needlework to make them thoughtful of others."

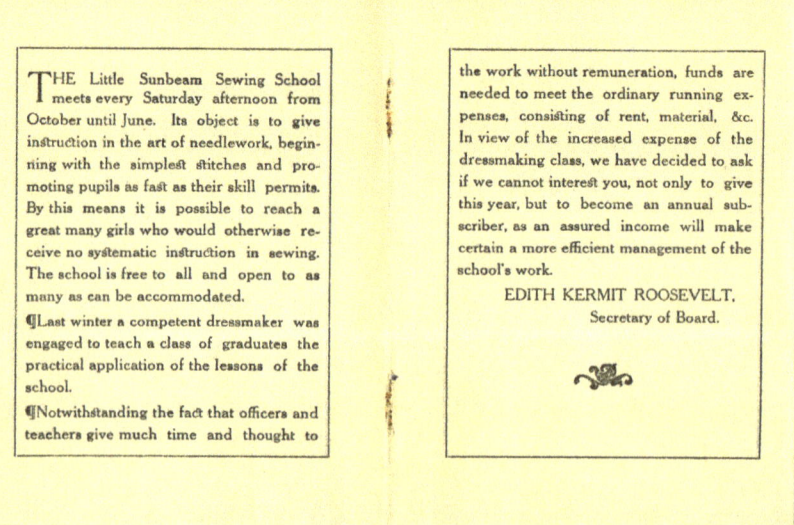

Courtesy of the Sagamore Hill National Historic Site, National Park Service, Oyster Bay, NY

Theodore was the uncle of FDR's wife Eleanor Roosevelt.

The collection of First Ladies China in the Smithsonian's National Museum of American History was made possible because of Edith.

After reading the biography of the poets Elizabeth and Robert Browning, Edith burned all of her correspondence with her husband. She didn't want her private life to be made public. Her daughter Ethel Roosevelt Derby saved four letters from the flames, and they were found in trunks in the attic after Ethel died in her Oyster Bay, Long Island home in 1977.

This is an excerpt from a letter Teddy wrote to her from East Africa: "You have made the real happiness of my life and so it is natural and right that I should constantly be more and more lonely without you."

Edith died in her bed on September 30, 1948 at Sagamore Hill which she left to the nation. Her only surviving child, Ethel, was on its board of directors until she died.

Sagamore Hill looks manly with its bear skin rugs and mounted wild animals. Edith's drawing room (or parlor room), however, upon entrance on the left captures her personality with its pastel colors, petite desk for writing and bill paying, and shelves of books. She did not let Theodore or his guests sit in her room.

You can visit Sagamore Hill in Oyster Bay, Long Island. The couple is buried nearby at Young Cemetery.

VISIT:

**Sagamore Hill
20 Sagamore Hill Road
Oyster Bay, NY 11771**

Explore 83 acres of natural surroundings and historic buildings.

nps.gov/sahi

**In the Works:
The Theodore Roosevelt Presidential Library
North Dakota**

trlibrary.com

The Roosevelts lived in Sagamore Hill, a large home in Oyster Bay, Long Island. It became known as the "Summer White House." People still visit it today.

Courtesy of *the Sagamore Hill National Historic Site, National Park Service, Oyster Bay, NY*

Edith Roosevelt's Knitting Pattern for Men's Socks

14 in leg. 11 1/2 in f ot.

MRS. THEODORE ROOSEVELT, SENIOR
SAGAMORE HILL
OYSTER BAY, NEW YORK

Men s Socks.

Set up 64 stitches on 3 needles. Rib 5 in deep, k.2 purl2. Knit for 7 in. more which brings you to heel. Divide stitches equally, 32front, 32 back needle. K. heel stockin ettstitch, then turn. Pick up stitches on R. side of heel, about 15. K. across front. Pick up same unmber of stitches on left side. K. once round. Narrow every other round on next to last stich of back needles. (Front ends) Narrow until 64 stitches on all 3 needles. Knit foot to within 3 in of desired length, narrow for toe, finish.

Turn heel. When required depthpurl half the no. of stitches, p. 2 more. p. 2 together. p.1, turn. Slip 1 stitch. k.5. k.2 together, k.1 turn and purl across to the hold made by slipping the stitch. p. stitches on each side of hole together, p.1. Repeat this always slipping 1 st. nd knitting or purling the 2 togehter each side of the hole until all the stitches on the needle are used up.

Double heel. Always slip first stitch. Purl over. Knit and slip alternately on knit side, slipping the slipped stitch as for purling.

To narrow for the toe.
Allow about 3 in in the length of foot for narrowing. Divide stitches, half for fromt needle, and quarter each for back needles. Narrow 4 times in a round. On the 3rd stitch from eache end of the frount needle and on 3rd stitch from front end of each back needle. K.4 rounds narrow sma eplace, 3 rounds and narrow, 3 rounds and narrow, 2 rounds and narrow, 2 rounds and narrow. 1 round and narrow, Now ev. round until 8 st. left front, 4 each back.

Give it a try. Good luck!

Kitchener toe.
8 st. on each needle. 2 needles. Hold 2 needles side by side thread coming from r. hand end of back needle. Break off wool about 10 in. from sock, thread on darning needle pull through last stitch on front needle as if knitting, slip stitch off. Pull thread through 2nd stitch of front needle as if purling and leave stitch on needle. Pull thread through first stitch of back needle as if purling, slip stitch off. Pull through 2nd st. as if knitting and leave on. Repeat from beginning until finished.

HELEN HERRON TAFT

First Lady of Potomac Park

Helen "Nellie" Taft loved Asian culture and the piano. After high school, she studied at the Cincinnati College of Music and later taught piano and helped found the Cincinnati Symphony Orchestra. Helen fell in love with Asia when she visited and lived in China, Japan, and the Philippines when she was younger.

When Nellie and her husband, President William Howard Taft, moved into the White House, Nellie wanted to share her love of the Asian culture and create a place to bring people together through the universal language of music. She began by decorating the rooms of the White House to look like China, Japan, and the Philippines. Nellie had furniture from the Philippines including chairs, beds, and a chest.

Then she envisioned a place where all Washington D.C. could meet, whether walking or driving, to concerts at 5:00 p.m. on certain evenings. She imagined Potomac Park could be something like the Luneta in the Philippines, one of the largest parks in Asia.

To attract people to Potomac Park, Nellie invited the Philippine Constabulary Band to play on opening day, April 17, 1909, which previously played on Taft's inauguration and at the 1904 World's Fair.

As Nellie watched the band in her signature Japanese geisha hairstyle, she noticed how Potomac Park looked just like the Luneta in the Philippines. It was also set by the bay and people could listen to music and see their neighbors just like at Luneta. Nellie achieved her goal of bringing people from different cultures together through the power of music.

Nellie also shared another wonderful memory of her travels in Asia with the American people.

Eliza Ruhamah Scidmore, an ambitious woman like Nellie, first spotted the cherry blossom trees in Tokyo in 1885. Eliza was an author and the first female board member of the National Geographic Society, and she wanted to have cherry blossom trees in America. So did a botanist named David Fairchild who was working in the newly created

Helen Taft loved Asian culture. She wore her hair Geisha-style and danced at the Inaugural Ball in a white satin gown she had sent to Tokyo, Japan to have embroidered with goldenrod flowers, outlined in silver.

Helen Taft is the first First Lady to have donated her gown to the Smithsonian Museum. This began the tradition for future first ladies to do the same.

Cherry Blossoms around the Tidal Basin, with the Washington Monument in the background

Smithsonian Institution Archives, Record Unit 7355, Martin A. Gruber Photograph Collection, SIA2010-2096

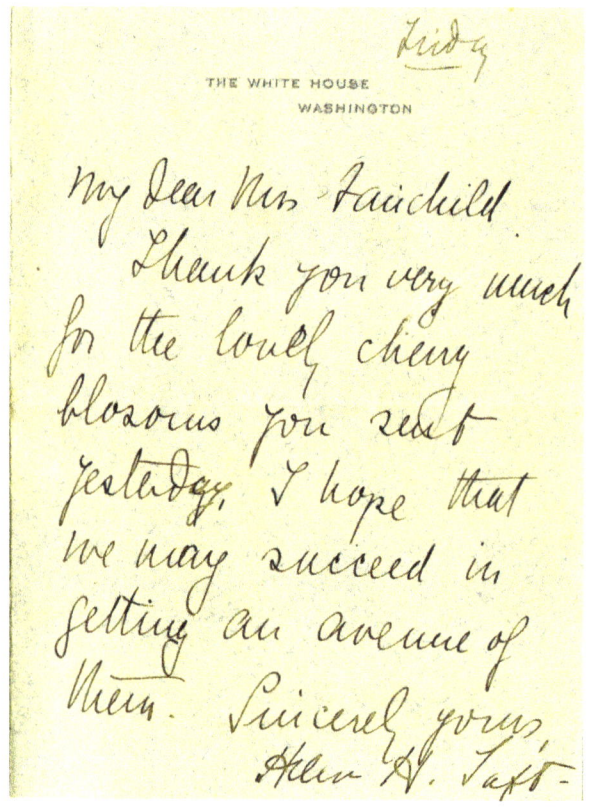

Courtesy of the First Ladies' Library

A letter written by Helen Taft to Mrs. Fairchild, thanking her for sending cherry blossoms. The Fairchilds supported Helen Taft's vision.

Office of Foreign Seed and Plant Introduction. David thought they would add beauty to the muddy banks along the Potomac.

Mrs. Scidmore wrote to Nellie about planting the cherry blossom trees around the Tidal Basin, which is a partially man-made reservoir between the Potomac River and the Washington Channel. The First Lady loved the idea, but she changed the design to make it look like it does today. How beautiful the city of Washington D.C. would become!

When Yukio Ozaki, the mayor of Tokyo, Japan, learned of this, he sent Nellie more than 2,000 cherry blossom trees as a gift to the American people in 1910. Unfortunately, the trees came with a disease and had to be burned. Two years later, approximately 3,000 trees were donated. On March 27, 1912, Nellie and the Japanese ambassador's wife, Iwa Chinda, planted the first two trees.

Nellie wrote a memoir called "Recollections of Full Years," and she said that she wanted to have a whole season of Japanese Cherry Blossoms in Potomac Park.

The Cherry Blossom Festival runs every year from March through April to commemorate the gift and to celebrate the friendship between the Japanese and the American people. The names of trees in Potomac Park are Yoshino Cherry, Akebono Cherry, Weeping Cherry, and other blooming trees like magnolias, dogwoods, red bud, and Japanese crab apples.

Hundreds of thousands visit each year to see and photograph the pink and white blooms near the Washington Monument and Jefferson Memorial. They also gather around the bandstand at Potomac Park and listen to world-class music.

The cherry blossom tree planted by Nellie is still there, marked by a plaque.

The Cherry Blossom Festival runs every year from March through April.

Courtesy of the Author

Needlework by Helen Taft

The new Mrs. Taft took up the challenge of homemaking with her characteristic enthusiasm. The young couple had a house built on McMillan Street. As part of the furnishings for that house, she is reported to have done the needlework on this chair.

Courtesy of William Howard Taft National Historic Site

HELEN HERRON TAFT
First Lady to 27th President (1909 – 1913)

Helen Taft
c. 1909
Library of Congress cph.3a53353

Mrs. Taft in Filipina costume

Library of Congress ds.04248

Helen Herron Taft was born on June 2, 1861 in Cincinnati, Ohio to parents John Herron and Harriet Collins Herron. Her father was a state senator. She was the fourth of 11 children. Helen's younger sister, Lucy Hayes Herron, was named after First Lady Hayes and christened at the White House and that's when Nellie first visited the White House.

Nicknamed Nellie, she was anxious, and the term "Nervous Nellie" came to be.

Nellie attended Miss Nourse's School. An accomplished pianist, she studied at Miami of Ohio University and then took classes at the Cincinnati College of Music.

Nellie Taft was once a kindergarten teacher. Nellie taught sewing, drawing, piano, French, and grammar at private schools until she became a mother.

Nellie dreamed of living in the White House and also wanted to be a lawyer. But her father told her that if she became a lawyer nobody would want to marry her. So she married one.

His name was William Howard Taft. He earned a degree at Yale University and a law degree from Cincinnati Law School in Ohio. William had a dream too. He wanted to become a Supreme Court Justice.

They married on June 19, 1886 in her parents' home. She was 25, and he was 29.

The couple had three children: Robert, Helen and Charles.

On March 4, 1909, a blizzard turned Washington, D.C. into a snowy and slushy mess which caused William's Inauguration Ceremony to be held inside the Senate Chambers of the Capitol. Nellie rode into the White House, alongside her husband President Taft in a 1909 White Steam Car that sounded like a big sewing machine. Nellie took her "rightful place," next to him — and not behind, as she said. The first First Lady to do so!

That evening, President and First Lady Taft danced at the Inaugural Ball. Although a heavy man (nearly 350 pounds), President Taft was a great dancer.

Her son Charles Taft became Mayor of Cincinnati. Helen Taft Manning became a professor of history, a college dean, and was outspoken on women's rights. Robert Taft served in the Senate from 1939 until 1953.

She was the most well-traveled first lady upon entering the White House.

As first lady, Nellie invited all people to the White House including African Americans, divorced people, Native Americans, and new immigrants. At her 25th wedding anniversary party, Nellie invited leaders from all faiths. She grew up Episcopalian.

In 1900, President McKinley asked Taft to become Civil Governor of the Philippines, which was an American property until July 4, 1946. She started the "Drop of Milk" nutritional program for infants.

After President McKinley was assassinated in 1901, President Theodore Roosevelt twice offered Taft an appointment to the Supreme Court, but Helen had him turn it down. She wanted her husband to be President. In 1921, President Warren Harding appointed Taft to the Supreme Court. Taft served in that capacity until one month before his death on March 8, 1930. Taft is the first and only President to have also served as a Supreme Court Justice.

Nellie hosted a private wedding ceremony for former First Lady Frances Cleveland's second marriage to Professor Thomas J. Reston, Jr. on February 10, 1913.

They were the first presidential couple to ride in a motorcar, and the last couple to have a cow graze upon the White House lawn.

She was the first First Lady to attend a Supreme Court argument and the first to attend a political convention. She is also the first First Lady to write an autobiography, but the book called "Recollections of Full Years" was not published until after Nellie died.

About two and a half months into her term on May 17, 1909, Nellie had a stroke while on the presidential yacht. After her stroke, Nellie couldn't even speak. President Taft missed her voice and her advice. She used to listen to the Cabinet meetings in the next room. She had to rely upon her sisters to represent her as hostess.

Although this slowed her down, Nellie lived to the age of 82 and died on May 22, 1943 in Washington D.C.

You can visit the William Howard Taft Historic Site in Cincinnati, Ohio. The couple is buried at Arlington National Cemetery in Virginia.

Nellie was the first First Lady to be buried at Arlington in Section 30. The only other First Lady buried there is Jacqueline Bouvier Kennedy Onassis.

VISIT:

**William Howard Taft National Historic Site
2038 Auburn Avenue
Cincinnati, OH 45219
nps.gov/wiho**

President rides in the motorcade

Courtesy of William Howard Taft National Historic Site

The William Howard Taft birthplace and house, part of the William Howard Taft National Historic Site in Cincinnati, Ohio.

Courtesy of William Howard Taft National Historic Site

EDITH BOLLING GALT WILSON

The Secret President

Not too long after President Wilson became a widower, Edith Bolling Galt visited a friend of President Wilson's for tea at the White House. President Wilson got a glimpse of her. Their eyes met in that stairwell, and as she would say, "I turned a corner and met my fate."

Then on December 18, 1915, Edith Bolling Galt became the second Mrs. Wilson and moved into the White House. It was nearing the end of President Wilson's term. Little did she know then that she would also become known as the Secret President.

Her husband President Wilson tried to keep peace. But the world was at war. Germany had sank a British luxury cruise ship called the Lusitania on May 7, 1915, and 124 American civilians lost their lives. Still, it took two years for President Wilson to declare war on April 2, 1917. After he delivered that message, he returned to his office and sobbed. He realized he had sent young soldiers to their deaths.

The War Effort

President Wilson presented a plan for peace, called Fourteen Points, on February 14, 1919. He envisioned a League of Nations. He wanted World War I to be the "war to end all wars."

To do her part in the war effort, Edith led by example. Not a time for celebrations, she cancelled all public tours of the White House. There would be no Easter Egg Roll or New Year's Day reception.

To encourage all to ration or do with less, she wore thrifty clothes and created "Meatless Mondays" and "Wheatless Wednesdays." She borrowed 20 sheep from a nearby farm to keep the White House lawn neat, which saved on gardening costs. The "White House Wool" originally earned $50,000 at auction and was given to the Red Cross for the war effort. Edith volunteered at the Red Cross Union Station to help the soldiers. She sewed pajamas, trench helmets, and blankets for them, too.

> **Edith brought her sewing machine to the White House.**
> She wrote in her memoir, "But in a little over a year when we entered the World War, the wheels of that machine seldom were idle as we turned out in stolen moments pajamas, surgical shirts, etc. for the Red Cross."

Smithsonian Institution Archives, Record Unit 7355, Martin A. Gruber Photograph Collection, SIA2010-1990

During World War I, Woodrow and Edith Wilson kept a flock of sheep on the White House grounds to save costs to cut the grass. The wool was also auctioned off to raise money for the Red Cross.

Smithsonian Institution Archives, Record Unit 7355, Martin A. Gruber Photograph Collection, SIA2010-1986

"Petticoat Government" is a term used for a government by women. A petticoat is an undergarment worn under a skirt or dress.

Women earned the right to vote when the 19th Amendment became a part of the United States Constitution on August 18, 1920.

Woodrow and Edith Wilson
National Portrait Gallery, Smithsonian Institution
S/NPG.76.39

Edith traveled with President Wilson across the country in the late summer of 1919 so that he could persuade the people to support his League of Nations. It was called the "whistle-stop tour," and President Wilson sometimes made three of his brilliant speeches in one day. This exhausting trip took a toll on him, and on September 25, he collapsed. On October 2, he suffered a stroke. Paralyzed on one side, his face drooped, and he grew a beard to hide it.

Edith wanted her husband to keep his job as President.

Instead of telling his Cabinet, the press, and the American people the truth about his condition, Mrs. Wilson told them he needed rest. At that time, there was no legislation in place stating that the vice-president would take over the office if the president would not be able to continue his work. Mrs. Wilson wanted to spare him the stress and save his life. Then she blocked the door and kept everyone away, except their good friend, Dr. Cary Grayson.

And this is how the second Mrs. Wilson became nicknamed the Secret President or the First Woman President or the Assistant President.

During this "Petticoat Government," Edith decoded military messages and read all of her husband's correspondence. She decided which she would bring to his attention. She didn't want to jeopardize his recovery, and she took matters into her own hands so her husband could maintain his presidency. She put her love for him above the responsibility to the American people.

Historians are still debating how much Edith, who had little formal education, actually did over those 13 months until the term ended.

She received the proposed State of the Union address and her handwriting was on those important papers. But in her memoir entitled "My Memoir" she wrote, "I myself never made a single decision regarding the disposition of public affairs."

One thing is certain. It will not happen again. The passage of the 25th Amendment of 1967 set rules on how to proceed if a president can no longer perform his job.

President Wilson gave Edith an orchid every day. On October 15, 2017, at a special reception at her birthplace, a purple orchid bred for her and named after her was unveiled.
It's called Lc Edith Bolling Wilson.

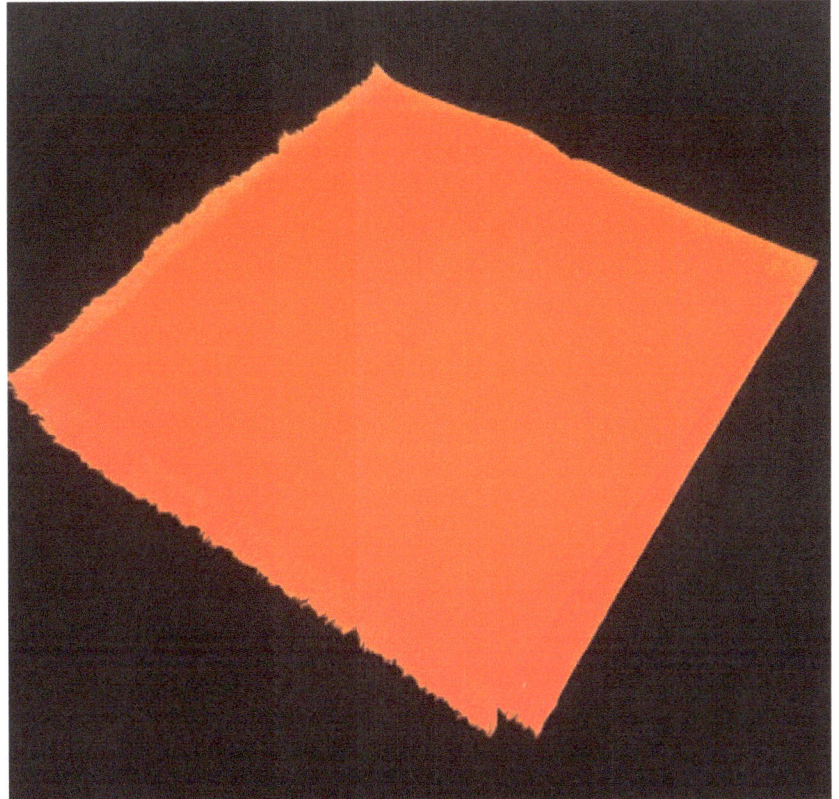

Courtesy of the Edith Bolling Wilson Birthplace Museum in Wytheville, Virginia

Mrs. Wilson was talented with needlepoint. She covered the dining room chairs in her home on S Street, but she preferred to make special gifts for her family such as this fringed napkin in orange.

Courtesy of the Edith Bolling Wilson Birthplace Museum in Wytheville, Virginia

Edith's "Grandmother Bolling," Anne Wigginton Bolling, taught Edith much of what she knew of domestic arts. They had a close relationship.

Portrait of Edith Wilson
by Emile Alexay

*National Portrait Gallery, Smithsonian Institution
NPG.69.43*

Historic Image of Edith's Home
Courtesy of the Edith Bolling Wilson Birthplace Museum in Wytheville, Virginia

EDITH BOLLING GALT WILSON
First Lady to (second wife of) 28th President (1915 – 1921)

Edith Wilson
*Library of Congress
cph.3a26698
between 1915 and 1921*

She was born on October 15, 1872 in Wytheville, Virginia to Circuit Court Judge William Holcombe Bolling and his wife Sallie White Bolling. Edith Bolling Galt Wilson is the first First Lady to come from Appalachia. She is also a descendant of Pocahontas.

Raised in a happy childhood home, she was the seventh of 11 children and very close with her grandmother. Although she had little formal education, she studied music at Martha Washington College for a semester and later spent a second year at the Powell School in Richmond. Shortly thereafter she married Norman Galt. With him, Edith had a baby boy in 1903, but the child died three days later. She then was unable to have children. After Norman's death, she helped to run his jewlery store, Galt & Bro. Jewelers. On March 8, 2001, it closed after nearly two centuries of continuous operation.

Her favorite designer, English-born Charles Frederick Worth, was the first to label his garments.

President Wilson's first wife Ellen was an artist, and she died during his first term in 1914. They had three daughters.

On December 18, 1915, Edith Bolling Galt became the second Mrs. Wilson. She wore a black velvet gown and a black velvet hat trimmed with feathers. She also wore an orchid pinned to her dress. They married in her home and then honeymooned in Hot Springs, Virginia.

In addition to baseball and politics, President Wilson loved to ride his bicycle. When he found out that Edith could not ride a bike, he tried to teach her. She practiced in the basement of the White House! She rode her bike into boxes and broke some china. That's when it was decided to give the china its own room in the White House.

Edith was the first First Lady to display china in 1917, and today every president is represented in the room.

She was the first honorary president of the Girl Scouts. In 1917, founder Juliette Gordon Low designed a "Thanks Badge" for Edith because she encouraged the newly formed group. Edith gifted this beautiful emerald and diamond back to the Juliette Gordon Low birthplace in Savannah, Georgia in 1958 where it is still on display.

The first First Lady to travel to Europe, she went with President Wilson in 1918 and in 1919 for the Treaty of Versailles in Paris which ended World War I. They were treated like royalty and even stayed at Buckingham Palace.

Edith is the only Southern Appalachian born First Lady.

She was the first honorary president of the Girl Scouts.

Edith was the first First Lady to travel to Europe.

President Wilson died at their home on 2340 S Street in Washington D.C. on February 3, 1924.

Edith spent the next 37 years honoring his memory and promoting his legacy for world peace. President Wilson is the only President to earn a PhD., which is a Doctor of Philosophy, (in political science from Johns Hopkins University.) He taught at Princeton University, served as its president, and was governor of New Jersey. President Wilson also won the Nobel Peace Prize in 1920 for his work on ending World War I and the creation of the League of Nations.

In 1904, Edith also became the first woman in Washington D.C. licensed to drive her own electric car. She drove a Columbia Elberon Victoria Mark XXXI. She was a foward-thinking woman for her time.

In 1938, Edith published "My Memoir."

She lived to ride in the Inaugural Parade for President John F. Kennedy and entertained First Lady Jacqueline Kennedy at her home with a luncheon.

Edith died at the age of 89 in her home on December 28, 1961 on the 105th anniversary of Woodrow Wilson's birthday. On that day, the Woodrow Wilson Bridge was commemorated with a ceremony that she was supposed to attend.

Until her death, Edith insisted that she never assumed presidential responsibility. She is buried with President Wilson at Washington National Cathedral. She did not like to be called First Lady. She preferred First Wife.

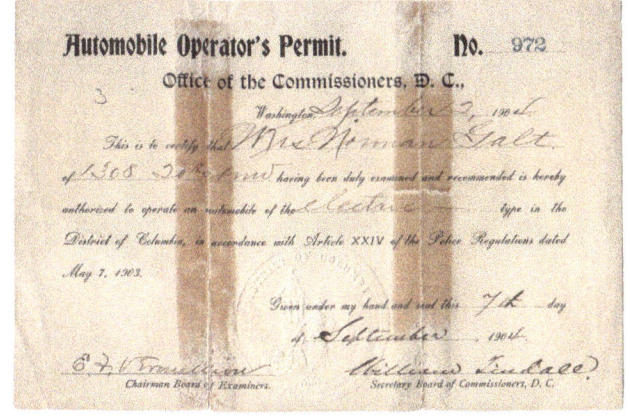

Courtesy of the Edith Bolling Wilson Birthplace Museum in Wytheville, Virginia

Edith's "automobile operator's permit" under her first married name, Mrs. Norman Galt.

VISIT:

**The Edith Bolling Wilson Birthplace Museum
145 E. Main Street
Wytheville, VA 24382**

edithbollingwilson.org

**The Woodrow Wilson House
2340 S Street
Washington D.C. 20008**

woodrowwilsonhouse.org

**Woodrow Wilson Presidential Library known as the "Manse"
20 N Coalter St.
Staunton, VA 24401**

woodrowwilson.org

Courtesy of the Edith Bolling Wilson Birthplace Museum (pictured here) in Wytheville, Virginia

FLORENCE MABEL KLING HARDING

Champion for Her Boys, the Veterans of World War I

On November 9, 1921 in the Capitol Rotunda, Florence Harding placed a white silk ribbon, one she had sewed herself, on the American-flag draped casket. Then her husband, President Warren G. Harding, placed a silver shield with 48 stars and a wreath of crimson roses on the coffin.

Vice President Calvin Coolidge placed a wreath of pink roses and snapdragons. Chief Justice of the Supreme Court William Howard Taft placed a wreath of chrysanthemums and carnations. And General Pershing who represented the "Father" of the "Unknown Boy" placed a wreath of giant pink chrysanthemums on the casket too.

Close to 100,000 Americans lined up to pay their last respects to this "Unknown Soldier" who lay in state for two days. All kinds of flowers came from all over the world.

On November 11, 1921, this unidentified American soldier who died in France during World War I was buried at Arlington National Cemetery in a memorial called the Tomb of the Unknown Solider. President Harding asked for a two-minute moment of silence from the thousands of people in attendance. He said, "We know not where he came, but only that his death marks him with everlasting glory of an American dying for his country."

First Lady Harding placed a wreath on the tomb on that Armistice Day. This tradition is done every Memorial Day and Veterans Day.

Florence also led the effort to sell red-dyed poppies to help raise funds for the veterans, which is also still done today.

Florence cared for the soldiers even before she became first lady. When her husband was serving as a United States senator during World War I, Florence worked at Washington's Union Station and brought coffee and reading materials to the soldiers.

When the soldiers came back from war, there were

> President Warren Harding once wrote in a letter that Florence and other senate wives had sewing sessions (using a sewing machine) in which they made bandages for soldiers.

Florence Harding standing with seven young men in uniform on the steps of her home in Marion, Ohio, in 1920 during the "front porch" presidential campaign for her husband Warren G. Harding.

Courtesy of the Ohio History Connection

Courtesy of the Ohio History Connection

Florence Harding with a young boy in a Marines hat, on the steps of her Ohio home in 1920.

questions to answer. What were they to do? Where would they go? How would they feel normal again?

"Normalcy" was the trademark term used during the Harding Administration, and Florence used her position as first lady to help veterans.

She called them "My Boys." If she saw one of her "boys," she would stop and make sure that he would have the help he needed. She volunteered as an aide at Walter Reed General Hospital. She shook many hands and cared for many hearts.

Florence established the White House Veterans Garden Party. She would invite her "boys" to the White House for sandwiches, cake, lemonade, and punch on the great lawn. They came on crutches, with canes, and in wheelchairs. They came blinded and bandaged. Florence made an effort to greet them all. One disabled veteran had given her a four-leaf-clover, and Florence put it in a locket. Another made her a tin box.

It is because of Florence's work in veterans' affairs that the first Veterans Bureau was established under the Harding Administration to help the veterans with their postwar care.

Florence was determined to make things better, and she

Florence with a soldier at Walter Reed General Hospital. She used her position as first lady to help veterans. (photo taken between 1921 and 1923.)

Library of Congress hec.30858

encouraged veterans' families to write to her about their problems. Florence would even make inspections of the facilities herself.

Florence was a compassionate person. She recognized the suffering in others, as she herself suffered greatly from a condition of the kidneys called nephritis. This caused her deep pain in her abdomen and caused her hands and feet to swell. She was bedridden for three or four months at a time. But in spite of her hardships, she persevered.

She not only cared for the veterans, but she also advocated on behalf of women, African Americans, prisoners, and animals. Florence and Warren had run a newspaper before entering politics, and she knew how to work with the media. She posed for photos that would tell the stories about her causes and influence public opinion.

Florence was the first First Lady to be in the White House after World War I ended. She was also the first woman to vote for her husband in a presidential election, the first First Lady to fly in an airplane, and the first to have been divorced.

Most of all, she and her husband President Warren G. Harding deeply appreciated the sacrifices made by veterans in the World War I, "the war to end all wars." She opened the door for future first ladies to use the position as a platform to fight for causes they believe in.

Florence was good with the press and at portraying different images, from homemaker to modern working woman, depending upon the audience.

One of the many roles she portrayed included her knitting on her front porch while giving an interview during the presidential campaign.

To appear as a homemaker, she passed out her waffle recipe and gave interviews.

Although Florence did know how to knit and do needlepoint, she was more interested in riding horses, playing the piano, and learning about music, art and business procedures.

Florence Harding shaking hands with a man seated on a bed.
(photo taken between 1920 and 1924) *Courtesy of Library of Congress cph.3c00077*

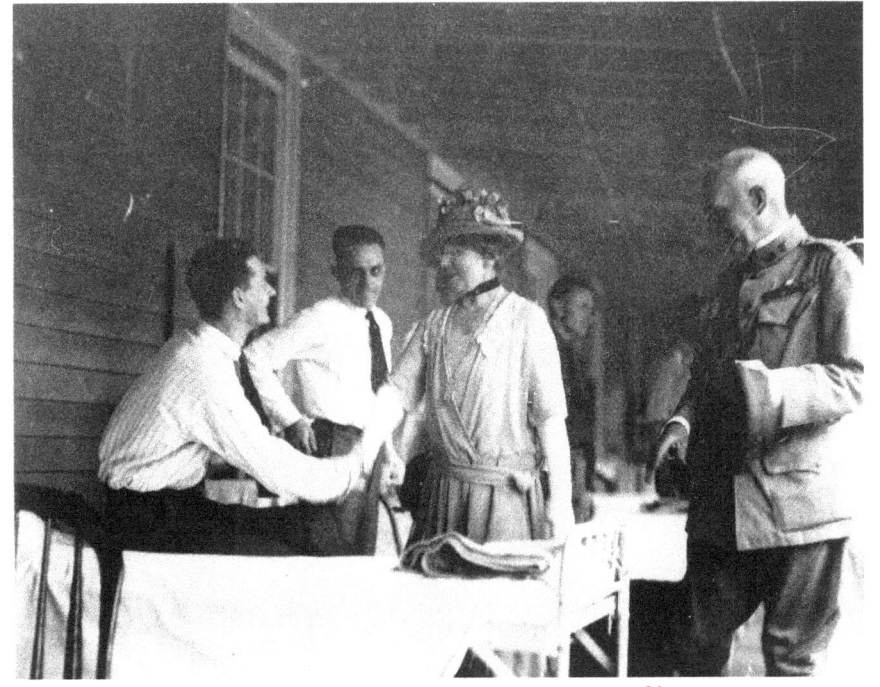

FLORENCE MABEL KLING HARDING
First Lady to 29th President (1921 – 1923)

Florence Harding
between 1920 and 1923
Library of Congress cph.3a09266

Florence Harding was a fierce advocate for women, African Americans, prisoners (especially women), animals, and veterans. Below, on her porch, two young girls give her a basket of flowers.

Courtesy of the Ohio History Connection

Florence Harding's influence may be felt today. Red poppies are still sold to raise money for veterans.
Courtesy of the Author

On August 15, 1860, Florence Mabel Kling was born. Her father, Amos Kling, was the richest man in their hometown of Marion, Ohio. Even though he had two sons after Florence, he raised his daughter to be independent. Her mother was Louise Mabel Hanford Bouton Kling.

Florence dreamed of becoming a concert pianist and studied at the Cincinnati Conservatory. She eloped with Henry DeWolfe, and they had a son, Eugene Marshall DeWolfe. But Henry suffered from alcoholism, and he abandoned them. Florence found herself a single mother, and to support herself and her son, she gave piano lessons to children in the neighborhood.

A few years later, Florence's father offered to adopt her son. Florence's role became more of an aunt than a mother. History recalls her as not being maternal, but her concern for veterans, whom she called her "boys," shows her softer side.

At the age of 30, she married Warren Gameliel Harding on July 8, 1891 in the home they had built in Marion. Warren was five years younger and a newspaper man. His newspaper the "Daily Star" became the "Marion Star," and Florence helped him run the business side of the paper. Her father had taught her well. She hired the paper boys and increased circulation rates.

Florence and Warren had no children together. Even though Warren was not faithful to Florence, she stayed by his side and was instrumental in helping him to become president of the United States. Florence once said that her only one real hobby was her husband. He called her "The Duchess."

Florence Harding was a fierce advocate for women, African Americans, prisoners (especially women), animals, and veterans. Camp Alderson, a federal prison camp for women to encourage reformation, was inspired by Florence's efforts.

She and her husband loved the movies. In the age of celebrity, she hosted many people at the White House, including Albert Einstein, Madame Curie, and Al Jolson. America fell in love with their dog Laddie Boy, an Airedale. She was good with the press and a master of photographic opportunities, known as photo ops.

She wore a color which became known as "Harding Blue" and a necklace like a choker called the "Flossy Kling," and she was known for her waffles. Florence was a champion of the Girl Scouts and favored women reporters. She was the first example of what a modern First Lady could be and could do.

Warren and Florence were traveling home from their Alaska trip called the "Voyage of Understanding," when on August 2, 1923, President Harding had a heart attack at the Palace Hotel in San Francisco. Florence rode with his body on a train all the way back to Washington D.C. for a state funeral and then ultimately to their hometown for the burial. Crowds had gathered to see the train pass, and they sang songs and hymns.

She died in Marion, Ohio on November 21, 1924. They are buried at the Harding Tomb, also called the Harding Memorial, in Marion, Ohio.

Florence Harding never wore a wedding ring because she thought it meant that she had to obey her husband. She was very independent. She did wear, however, a mourning ring, to show respect for her late husband.

The Harding Home Presidential Site is located at 380 Mt. Vernon Avenue in Marion, Ohio. The Harding Presidential Center, built alongside the Harding home, opened in 2020 to commemorate the 100th anniversary of the 1920 front porch campaign.

Warren and Florence Harding waving to a crowd of supporters on the steps of their Canton, Ohio home during the 1920 "front porch" presidential campaign.

Courtesy of Ohio History Connection

**Harding Home (above)
Presidential Library & Museum (below)**
Courtesy of the Harding Home Presidential Site

VISIT:

**The Harding Home Presidential Site
380 Mt. Vernon Ave.
Marion, OH 43302**

hardingpresidentialsites.org

GRACE ANNA GOODHUE COOLIDGE

The Cool Pennsylvania Avenue Zoo!

First Lady Grace Coolidge and her husband, President Calvin Coolidge, made a cool couple. He was shy, and she did much of the talking. And they both loved animals.

They had the most animals when they lived in the White House.

There were lots of cool dogs. Boston Beans, a bulldog; Calamity Jane, a sheepdog; Tiny Tim, a red chow; Peter Pan, a terrier; and Blackberry, a chow.

But the most famous dogs were two white collies named Rob Roy and Prudence Prim. Rob Roy sat in a chair next to the president and shared his cereal every morning. Rob Roy also attended weekly press conferences, and Prudence Prim never left the First Lady's side. Grace even made Prudence Prim a straw bonnet to wear at a White House garden party.

There were lots of cool cats too: Tiger; Blacky; Smoky; and Bounder. President Coolidge would hide Smoky and Bounder in different places around the White House. Grace would always listen for Bounder's pleading meow and rescue her.

There were lots of cool birds too. And they were allowed to fly around in the White House. Nip and Tuck, yellow canaries; Snowflake, a white canary; and Old Bill, a thrush.

Grace even had a mockingbird for a short time until she found out it was illegal to own one.

But Grace's favorite bird was Do-Funny. Do-Funny came from South America and did funny things. Do-Funny would eat right out of Grace's mouth and whistle and sing along with her.

Kind people from all over the world started to send cool animals to the White House.

One Easter, 13 Pekin Ducklings arrived, and Grace tried to raise the ducklings in one of the White House bathrooms.

There was Enoch, a goose; and Ebeneezer, a donkey.

The newspapers reported that the Coolidges had their own cool zoo on Pennsylvania Avenue!

Things got a bit crazy. A black bear was trucked in from Mexico. A wallaby (that's a small kangaroo) flew in from Australia. And a small hippopotamus and lion cubs traveled all the way from South Africa. But these animals were too exotic to stay at the Pennsylvania Avenue Zoo, so the Coolidges took them to the zoo at nearby Rock Creek Park.

Things got even more interesting one November day in 1927. That's when a raccoon arrived on the doorstep of the White House, all the way from Mississippi, for Thanksgiving dinner.

The admirer did not send the raccoon to be a guest at the Thanksgiving Day table. Oh, no. The raccoon was sent to be on the table… instead of the turkey!

First Lady Grace Coolidge holding a bird at the White House

Library of Congress hec.43647

Luckily, the President and the First Lady welcomed the raccoon into their home and let her roam around the place. They even gave her a collar on Christmas day with her name, Rebecca Racoon of the White House.

Rebecca took over. She ran up and down the White House halls. She dug up houseplants. She unscrewed lightbulbs. She ripped up the fabric on the furniture, and she even destroyed some clothes.

Rebecca took long baths and played with a cake of soap. Grace fed her shrimp and persimmon, which is a fruit. And the Coolidges made Rebecca her own home in a tree outside the President's office. President Coolidge even walked her on a leash on the Great Lawn. She was so spoiled.

To calm her down, the Coolidges chose Reuben the Raccoon to be Rebecca's husband. But Reuben did an uncool thing and ran away.

One Easter Monday in 1927, the First Lady brought Rebecca to the White House Easter Egg Roll on the Great Lawn. As Grace hugged Rebecca tightly, Rebecca delighted tens of thousands of children that day and hundreds of photographers clicked away. That was Rebecca's most famous moment!

That summer Rebecca went on vacation to the Black Hills in South Dakota with the presidential couple and five canaries and Rob Roy and Prudence Prim. But Rebecca broke out of her cage and climbed the tallest pine tree. The Secret Service agents had to coax her down.

After that, Calvin and Grace decided that Rebecca's behavior was not cool, even for them. They brought her to the real zoo at Rock Creek Park where she joined many of the other animals who had been gifted to them from all around the world.

When President and First Lady Hoover moved into the White House, the Coolidges moved out and took all of their animals with them.

That's when the coolest thing happened.

Billy Possum, adopted by the Hoovers, moved into the old home of Rebecca Raccoon of the White House.

Grace Coolidge, two dogs, policemen and children at the White House Easter Egg Roll on April 13, 1925
Library of Congress cph.3c11726

Grace Coolidge and her dogs
Courtesy of the Vermont Historical Society

First Lady Grace Coolidge and Rebecca the Raccoon delight the children at the White House Easter Egg Roll.
Courtesy of the Vermont Historical Society

GRACE ANNA GOODHUE COOLIDGE
First Lady to 30th President (1923 – 1929)

Grace Coolidge
1923
Library of Congress cph.3c31581

Grace Coolidge could sew, knit and crochet. She crocheted the blanket for the Lincoln Bedroom in the White House in 1927.

Grace Anna Goodhue Coolidge was born on January 3, 1879 in Burlington, Vermont. She was an only child to parents Captain Andrew Issachar Goodhue and Lemira Barrett Goodhue.

At the age of 16, she decided to convert from Methodist to the Congregational Church.

Grace graduated from the University of Vermont in 1897. Always sociable and friendly, she began a sorority called Pi Beta Phi. She worked as a teacher of the deaf at the Clarke School for the Deaf before she was married.

On October 4, 1905, she married Calvin John Coolidge who was born on July 4, 1872. They married in a small ceremony in her parents' Vermont home.

The Coolidges had two sons, John and Calvin, Jr. Calvin died at age 16 from an infection on July 7, 1924 while the couple was in the White House.

She served as the First Lady of the United States of America from 1923 until 1929, before the Great Depression. President Calvin Coolidge took office upon the sudden death of President Warren Harding.

Grace had a lifelong interest in the hearing impaired and disabled community. She served on the board of directors of the Clarke School of the Deaf, alongside then United States Senator John F. Kennedy. She later served as its president from 1935 until 1952. She invited people with disabilities to visit the White House and Helen Keller was her favorite.

Grace Coolidge wrote poetry, and was published in "Good Housekeeping" magazine. An avid crafter, she also published patterns in ladies' magazines. Her mother had taught her how to knit, crochet and sew. She crocheted the blanket for the Lincoln bedroom in the White House in 1927.

Nicknamed the First Lady of Baseball, Grace was a Boston Red Sox fan. While in Washington D.C., she cheered

Courtesy of Vermont History Museum

Grace Coolidge and Helen Keller in The Detroit News

Courtesy of Library of Congress det.4a27973

for the Nationals and kept her own scorecard. She was also an expert swimmer, and loved to take long walks, play tennis and ice skate.

She played piano and was the most frequent theater-goer and loved to watch movies. The presidential yacht, the Mayflower, was rigged with a movie screen.

As First Lady, Grace rescued and restored antiques from the White House and renovated the third floor with a sky parlor to add more sunshine.

The Secret Service named her Sunshine. She read biographies of previous first ladies, and baked muffins, custards, and pies. She loved to dance the Charleston, but President Coolidge would not allow her to do so in public. She did so in private with her son John. Although President Coolidge, also known as "Silent Cal," was frugal, he enjoyed buying Grace elegant clothing.

The artist Howard Chandler Christy painted her portrait which hangs in the Red Room of the White House. She is wearing a red dress and Rob Roy, the white collie, is by her side. Rob Roy was fed candy to sit still.

VISIT:

Calvin Coolidge Presidential Library and Museum Forbes Library
20 West St.
Northampton, MA 01060

forbeslibrary.org

Vermont History Center
60 Washington St. Suite 1
Barre, VT 05641-4209

vermonthistory.org

Vermont History Museum
109 State St.
Montpelier, VT 05609

Coolidge Burial Site Plymouth Notch Cemetery
Plymouth, VT 05056

Grace Coolidge and Rob Roy

Library of Congress cph.3g06416

Courtesy of Vermont Historical Society (below)

LOU HENRY HOOVER

Courtesy of the Herbert Hoover Presidential Library from Iowa Historical Society

The President's Mountain School

Lou Henry Hoover's father wanted a boy. But when he had a baby girl, he gave her a boy's name and told her she could do anything she wanted to do. And Lou did.

She earned her A.B. degree in geology from Stanford University. Lou once said she wished it stood for "A" "Boy" because then she would have been able to get a job as a geologist. It was hard because she was the first woman at the school, and in the country, to graduate with a degree in that field in 1898.

Lou grew up a tomboy and when she married Herbert Hoover, Lou continued to camp, fish, and ride horses. Multi-millionaires by the time they were in the White House, President and First Lady Hoover purchased land with their own money in the Blue Ridge Mountains of Virginia, 100 miles away from Washington D.C. and high enough to avoid mosquitoes. They wanted a place where they could enjoy the weekends during the summer and the fall. They assigned the United States Marines to build it, and they promised to donate the 164 acres back to the government for future presidents to use as a retreat.

They called it Rapidan Camp after the Rapidan River, known for its trout fishing. Rapidan Camp was President Hoover's favorite pastime, and Lou was its main designer.

The Hoovers invited many people to go camping with them, including celebrities such as Thomas Edison and Charles Lindbergh. Only two years earlier, Lindbergh became famous for his nonstop flight from Long Island, New York to Paris, France.

Most of the time, the White House doctor, Colonel Joel Boone, came along and rode horseback along the trails. One day, Dr. Boone met a poor boy, 12 years of age, in the woods. The boy lived with his family in a nearby cabin. When President Hoover learned about the boy, he wanted him to visit the camp. President Hoover had been an orphan and cared about children. He promised to pay the boy $5 for a live possum.

On President Hoover's 55th birthday, the boy came out of the woods carrying a possum in a soap box covered in chicken wire. His name was Ray Buracker. President Hoover gave Ray $5 for the possum, which was a lot of money in those days. He introduced the boy to Lindbergh, but Ray never heard of the famous pilot or his transatlantic flight.

Mr. and Mrs. Hoover seated on wicker chairs in 1929.

Library of Congress cph.3c31568

President Hoover asked Ray where he went to school. Ray told President Hoover that there was no school for the kids on Doubletop Mountain. He didn't know how to read or write. Ray had never left the mountain.

The President and First Lady were shocked. Here they had been enjoying the mountains, while poor families were suffering in poverty nearby. How would the families survive? What would the children do? How would they learn to take care of themselves in the world?

The Hoovers knew that education was the answer, and they created the President's Mountain School.

The schoolhouse would have a community center and an apartment for a teacher. Lou would find the right person. She hired Christine Vest, a recent graduate of Berea College in Kentucky. Ms. Vest had experience teaching in a similar setting.

The Hoovers paid for most of the school and only required that it be built by local men in the community. The newspapers heard about the story, however, and people from all over the country sent donations. By the time the Hoovers left the White House in 1933, they had personally spent $24,000 on the school. That was a ton of money in those days, especially during the Great Depression which happened after the stock market crashed in late October of 1929.

The school opened on February 24, 1930, and 17 children attended. Ray and his five siblings and neighbors were ready to learn how to read and write and do arithmetic. Ms. Vest taught them how to manage their time and their money and how to order goods. She also took them to the Madison County Fair.

For the children, it was their first time off the mountain. At the fair, Ray and his siblings and classmates could go on all rides for as many times as they wanted. Ms. Vest wrote in one of her weekly letters to the White House, "We saw alligators, cowboys, ponies for the first time, the merry-go-round, turkey-geese, had red lemonade and carried balloons home!"

The school later held classes for adults, and Lou frequently visited. She also invited the children to have lunch at the White House. Lou wanted them to know that with an education they could do anything they wanted to do, too.

At the end of his administration and as promised, President Hoover donated Rapidan Camp to the government. But by 1935, though, all of the mountain cabins were knocked down and the families, including Ray Buraker, had to find new homes. The President's School closed, too. The Camp became

Lou Henry Hoover visits the schoolchildren at the President's Mountain School.
Courtesy of the Herbert Hoover Presidential Library and Museum

Mrs. Hoover hired Christine Vest (above), a recent graduate of Berea College in Kentucky, to be the teacher at the President's Mountain School (below). When the roads were bad in winter, she walked.

part of the Shenandoah National Park.

In an interview Ms. Vest, the teacher, said she felt a sense of accomplishment because Buraker was better able to take care of himself and his family.

Ray Buraker became known as the "possum boy." When he was 22, he enlisted in the Army during World War II. He worked in the field of electronics and lived to be 85 years old. Most of the other children went on to live ordinary lives.

Every letter that Lou received from the public asking for help from 1929 until 1933 was answered. Everybody was helped with the exception of about 1% of the letters that were thought to be phony. There were more letters after the Great Depression. Her social secretaries couldn't handle it with their other duties, so First Lady Hoover had hired her own personal secretary to handle the correspondence.

Lou was private and didn't talk about her good deeds. It wasn't until much after her death that the nation learned more from her scrapbooks, letters, and journals. The President had them sealed for 20 years.

After the school was demolished, people still wrote to Lou, asking for financial help to continue their studies. As they succeeded, people had been trying to repay her for years. She never told her husband. President Hoover discovered uncashed checks in her papers.

The schoolhouse was moved to Big Meadows on Skyline Drive. Today it serves as a ranger station in Shenandoah National Park.

Images Courtesy of the Herbert Hoover Presidential Library and Museum

LOU HENRY HOOVER
First Lady to 31st President (1929–1933)

Lou Henry Hoover

Images Courtesy of the Herbert Hoover Presidential Library and Museum

Lou served as Commissioner of the Girl Scouts. Athletic, she could camp, fish, ride horses, play baseball, and ice skate. She also knitted and supported the American Red Cross.

Lou Henry Hoover was born on March 29, 1874 in Waterloo, Iowa to parents Charles Delano Henry, a banker, and Florence Ida Ward Henry, a schoolteacher.

While a student she wrote an essay called, "An Independent Girl." Lou's family moved to California in 1884. She attended San Jose Normal School (now California State University) and earned a teaching certificate in 1893. A year later she went on to study at Stanford University.

It was hard because she was the first woman at the school, and even in the country, to graduate with a degree in geology in 1898. She met her future husband, Herbert ("Bert") Clark Hoover in a geology lab. The couple married on February 10, 1899. The day after they married, they left for China for his new job as a mining engineer.

She could speak Mandarin Chinese fluently, as well as other languages. While there, the Boxer Rebellion, an anti-Western uprising, took place. For the next years, the couple traveled the world and collected many items from different countries.

The couple translated a medieval encyclopedia on mining and metallurgy called "De Re Metallica" from Latin to English. The Mining and Metallurgical Society awarded them the Gold Medal for lifetime achievement.

They had two sons Herbert Charles and Allan Henry.

The family lived in London when World War I began in 1914. Lou helped her husband organize war relief efforts. She established the American Women's War Relief Fund and the American Women's Hospital. She also helped found the Food Administration Women's Club which helped young single women to find work in the new war agencies.

A big believer in athletics and outdoor activities for women, it is no wonder that the Girl Scouts appealed to Lou Henry Hoover. She was named commissioner in 1917 and in 1921 became vice president. From 1922 until 1925, she served as president and remained active with the Girl Scouts for the rest of her life.

Lou also created the Women's Division of the National Amateur Athletic Federation and chaired it from 1923 until 1927 and served as an honorary chair until 1941. Her mission was to encourage girls and young women to engage in physical and outdoor activities. Athletic, Lou could ride horses, fish, camp, play baseball, basketball, and ice skate. She organized the first National Conference on Athletics

and Physical Education for Women and Girls.

Lou was the first First Lady to broadcast a radio address. She delivered 15 of them and always supported her husband's causes. Yet, she kept her distance from reporters, and the public really didn't get to know how compassionate and kind she was. She was a Quaker and encouraged women to pursue public service.

During the Great Depression, Lou responded to many requests and spent her own money to aid those in need.

At Rapidan Camp, Lou Henry created 13 Camp Rules. General meetings were at the Town Hall, and the guests could play ping pong and knit. Lou was an excellent knitter and made baby blankets.

Lou died of a heart attack on January 7, 1944 in New York City. She is considered among historians to be the first modern First Lady.

Today Rapidan Camp is a National Historic Landmark at Shenandoah Park.

Franklin Delano Roosevelt could not enjoy Camp Rapidan because it was not wheelchair accessible. He built Shangri-La in the mountains of Western Maryland which later became known as Camp David, which is still the country retreat for presidents today.

Baby Blanket (above) and Scarf (below) knitted by Lou Henry Hoover

The Chippendale style mahogany screen features a cross-stitch needlework of the Washington Monument in shades of blue and white and initialed LHH (Lou Henry Hoover), dated 1932.

Courtesy of the Herbert Hoover Presidential Library and Museum

To learn more about the Hoovers, you can also visit the Herbert Hoover Presidential Library & Museum in West Branch, Iowa. The site contains gravesites of President and First Lady Hoover, an 81-acre park of tall grass prairie, the cottage where Herbert Hoover was born, the Friends meetinghouse where the family worshiped, several homes of the era and the Hoover Presidential Library Association.

VISIT:

The Herbert Hoover National Historic Site
110 Parkside Drive
West Branch, IA 52358

The Herbert Hoover Presidential Library & Museum
210 Parkside Drive
West Branch, IA 52358

hoover.gov

Courtesy of the Herbert Hoover Presidential Library (pictured here)

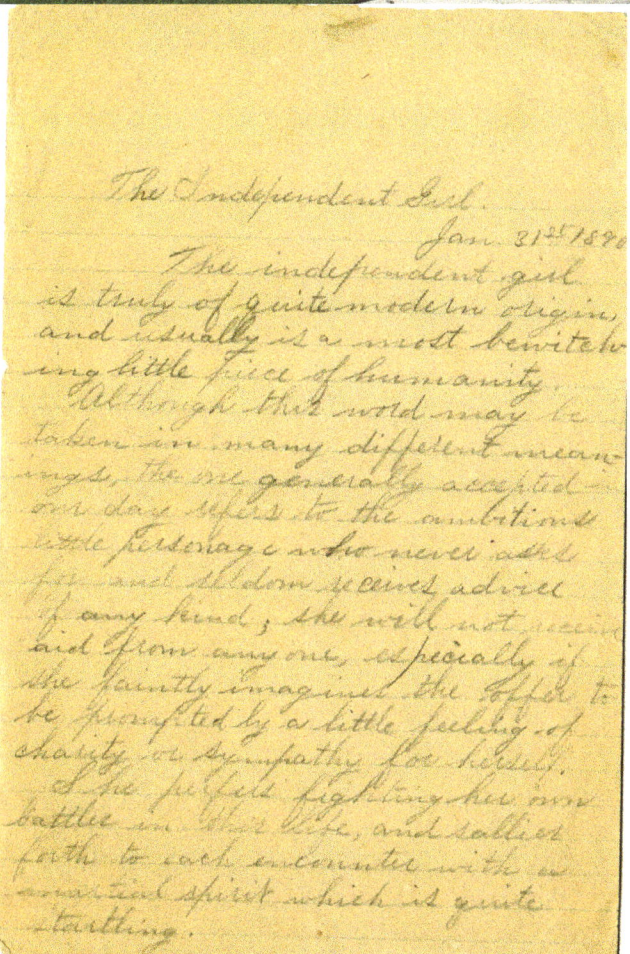

Excerpted from Lou Henry Hoover's January 31, 1890 essay entitled, "The Independent Girl."

"The independent girl is truly of quite modern origin, and usually is a most bewitching little piece of humanity."

"She prefers fighting her own battles in this life, and sallies forth with each encounter with a martial spirit which is quite startling."

"The independent girl is a person before whose wrath only the most rash dare stand, and, then it must be confessed with much fear and trembling."

ELEANOR ROOSEVELT

Courtesy of National Portrait Gallery, Smithsonian Institution NPG.82.158

First Knitter of the Land

Eleanor Roosevelt could not sit still.

She wrote a daily column, spoke publicly, and championed causes for minorities and women and the poor. This was a woman with little time on her hands to spare.

And yet, wherever she went, she carried a big knitting bag.

Eleanor had to keep her hands busy, too. She knit on planes. She knit on trains. And she knit at political and social conventions. She always wanted to be of use. To have a purpose. To serve.

Whenever she had a moment to herself in the midst of her busy schedule, Eleanor knitted mittens, sweaters, and socks for family and friends. She would ask other knitters for patterns and share patterns with other knitters. And since she made items to be used, not many items survived. The items were used and discarded. That's exactly what she intended.

First Lady Eleanor Roosevelt served alongside her husband, President Franklin Delano Roosevelt, for a long 12 years. Although she had loved working for the Red Cross during World War I, her husband felt it would be too dangerous to send the First Lady overseas during World War II. She had four sons in the military by that time. Yet, she still wanted to be more useful.

Eleanor wanted to work with the Red Cross refugee relief efforts in Western Europe. She wanted to serve hot meals to children, hand out medical supplies, and warm clothing to survivors.

So she found something more she could do for the war effort at home.

On September 30, 1941, First Lady Eleanor Roosevelt

Eleanor Roosevelt always wanted to be of use, to have a purpose, to serve.

It has been said that whenever Eleanor was sitting, she was knitting.

Courtesy of the Franklin D. Roosevelt Presidential Library and Museum, Hyde Park, New York.

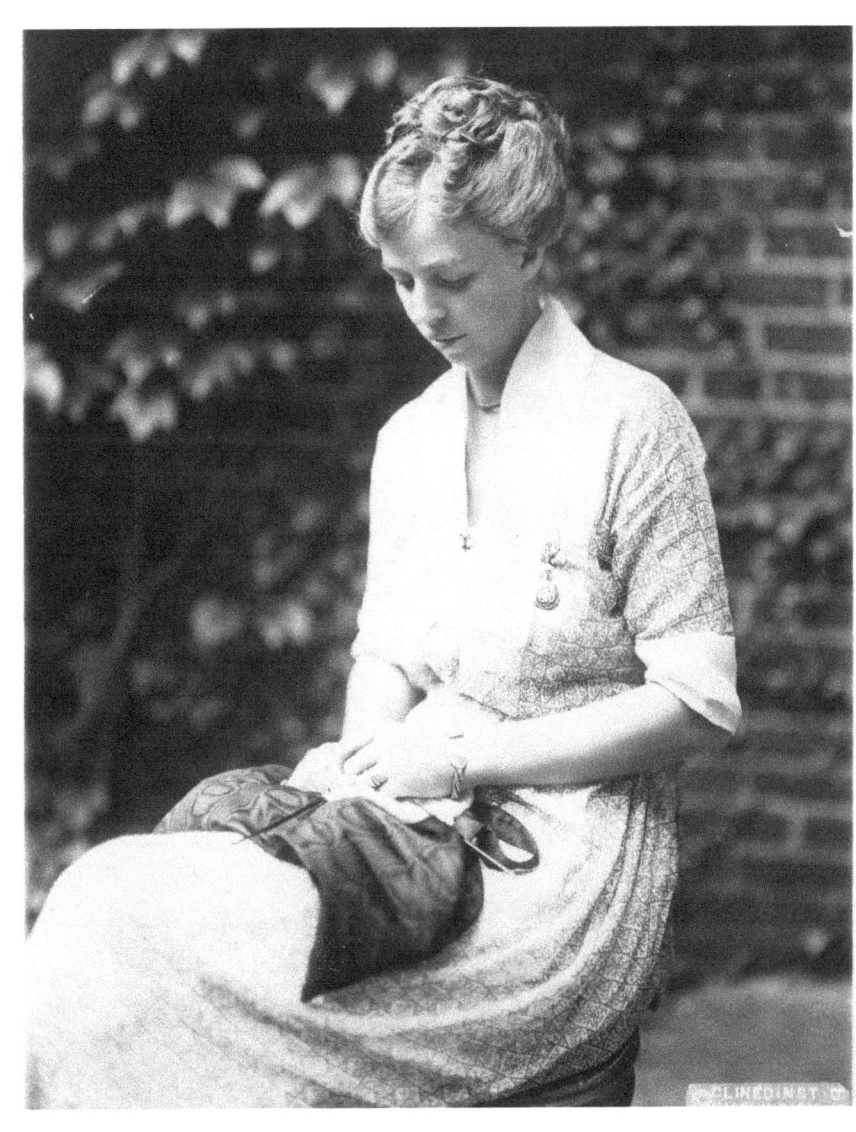

The cover story of LIFE magazine on November 24, 1941 got the nation knitting to help the soldiers keep warm.

The Army sold official instructions with khaki green yarn at stores that participated in the effort.

Knitting was also a great way to calm fears and to relieve the anxiety of those waiting to hear from loved ones serving in the war.

This knitting bag belonged to Eleanor Roosevelt. The wool fabric is gray with interwoven blue strands of blue, red, yellow, green, beige and black to form a plaid design. The double loop handle passes through brass rings to close the bag. The lining is black silk. The bag contains a pair of wooden knitting needles.

Courtesy of the Franklin D. Roosevelt Presidential Library and Museum, Hyde Park, New York

took to the stage in the ballroom at the Waldorf Astoria Hotel in New York City. She told the audience of 2,000 women, "We cannot turn our backs on the needs of other people." And then she began to knit after her speech, to lead by example.

Eleanor launched a national drive to enlist every American woman in a knitting army. She encouraged volunteers to knit one million sleeveless sweaters for soldiers and sailors before Christmas.

At the tea, Major General Irving J. Phillipson, Commander of the Second Army Corps, assured the women that both the sweaters and the thought behind the gifts would be deeply appreciated by the men in uniform.

Now with Eleanor as the "First Knitter of the Land," knitting became a national movement and a way for Americans to express their patriotism.

On November 24, 1941, LIFE magazine published a cover story called, "How to Knit." To help the war effort, the pattern for a simple knitted vest was included inside. The completed sweater was to be sent, with the name and address of the knitter, to a local group of people collecting the items to be shipped to soldiers.

Although the United States was still considered a neutral country, many soldiers had been sent overseas after Germany invaded Poland in 1939. But two weeks after the LIFE magazine article, the Japanese Navy Air Service attacked Pearl Harbor on December 7, 1941 and caused the United States to formally enter World War II.

Americans picked up their needles and started knitting on breaks from their jobs. They knit in factories. In hospitals. At gas stations. At movie theaters. At childcare facilities. They knit in the evenings when they listened to war-time news on the radio. The Glen Miller Band played "Knit One, Purl Two."

This song, along with Eleanor's plea, inspired people's love of country and the soldiers. Knitted sweaters from devoted women in towns far away from the war also warmed the hearts of the soldiers who received them.

Why did the warm clothing have to be knitted? In those days, handmade woolen clothing was stronger than any other material. Knitting was also a great way to calm fears and to relieve the anxiety of those waiting to hear from loved ones serving in the war.

In addition to the sleeveless sweaters, Americans also knit gloves, socks, and caps to wear under helmets, as well as gloves. Armies needed to change socks often to keep their feet dry in order to prevent a condition called trench foot which could cause amputation or death. People also knit bandages from white cotton yarn that had to be sterilized before sent.

Even though Eleanor inspired America's knitting and helping hands, she wanted to do more. In 1942, President Roosevelt finally agreed to send her to England. Eleanor visited wounded American soldiers in hospitals. She also visited the South Pacific and the Caribbean.

In her honor, every year the "Eleanor Roosevelt Knit-In" takes place in May at the Franklin Delano Roosevelt Presidential Library and Museum in Hyde Park, New York. Attendees knit and crochet yarn blocks to be assembled into afghans and donated to Veterans' Administrations Hospitals, battered women's shelters, American troops here and overseas, and others in need.

Eleanor Roosevelt knitting in 1909, alongside her daughter Anna. Years later she would launch a national drive to enlist every American woman in a knitting army to knit one million sleeveless sweaters for soldiers and sailors before Christmas.

Courtesy of the Franklin D. Roosevelt Presidential Library and Museum, Hyde Park, New York

Eleanor Roosevelt made this green khaki plain knit, long-sleeved pullover sweater for Joseph P. Lash while he was in the U.S. Army during World War II.

Courtesy of the Franklin D. Roosevelt Presidential Library and Museum, Hyde Park, New York

Songs like
"Knit One, Purl Two"
inspired people
to knit to help the soldiers.

They would sing the lyrics:

This sweater my darling's for you,
while vigil you're keeping
through rain and storm,
this sweater will keep you warm.

ELEANOR ROOSEVELT
First Lady to 32nd President (1933 – 1945)

Eleanor Roosevelt was once introduced as "first knitter of the land" and was pictured on her Christmas card knitting.

She was born Anna Eleanor on October 11, 1884 in New York City to wealthy parents Elliott Roosevelt and Anna Rebecca Hall Roosevelt. She preferred to use her middle name and was orphaned by the time she was 10. Painfully shy and awkward, she lived with her strict grandmother, and her governess would cut holes in socks so Eleanor would learn how to mend them. At 15, she was sent to the Allenswood Boarding School in England where she thrived.

Her uncle, President Theodore Roosevelt, walked her down the aisle to marry her distant cousin, Franklin Delano Roosevelt (FDR) on March 17, 1905. They had six children: Anna Eleanor, James, Franklin Delano, Jr. (who died in 1909), Elliott, Franklin Delano, Jr. and John Aspinwall.

She actively participated in her husband's political career and became an important leader in the Democratic Party and a humanitarian in her own right. She championed civil rights. After FDR was stricken with polio, Eleanor encouraged him to keep going.

Eleanor Roosevelt
Courtesy of National Portrait Gallery, Smithsonian Institution NPG.82.158 bequest of Phyllis Fenner

Eleanor married Franklin Delano Roosevelt (FDR) on March 17, 1905.
Courtesy of National Portrait Gallery, Smithsonian Institution NPG.2007.268 gift of Francis A. DiMauro

When FDR became president in 1933, Eleanor was comfortable in politics. She would not accept the traditional role of the first lady. She visited bread lines and coal mines and reported on how the New Deal was affecting ordinary people. Eleanor held her own press conferences. Six days a week, she wrote a national, syndicated newspaper column called "My Day" that reached millions of Americans. She published an autobiography in 1937 called "This Is My Story."

After her husband's death on April 12, 1945, Eleanor thought the "story was over." It wasn't. President Harry S. Truman appointed her the first United States delegate to the newly formed United Nations in 1945. He called her the "First Lady of the World."

She helped to found UNICEF, the United Nations Children's Fund, and she chaired the United Nation's Human Rights Commission. Committed to equal justice for all, Eleanor felt the most important work of her life was the Universal Declaration of Human Rights which she supported and helped to get adopted, almost unanimously, in 1948.

Eleanor died on November 7, 1962 in Hyde Park, New York. She is buried alongside her husband in the Rose Garden of Springwood, once the Franklin Delano Roosevelt home and now a National Historic Site.

Val-Kill (Dutch for "waterfall-stream"), the cottage where she lived, is the only National Historic Site dedicated to a First Lady. In May 1977, President Jimmy Carter signed the bill creating the Eleanor Roosevelt National Historic Site "to commemorate . . . the life and work of an outstanding woman in American History."

Courtesy of National Portrait Gallery, Smithsonian Institution NPG.2011.77.7 gift of George R. Rinhart, in memory of Joan Rinhart

Eleanor Roosevelt inspired many people, including Amelia Earhart, the first woman to fly non-stop and solo across the Atlantic Ocean. The two became close friends. They supported each other's causes. Inspired by Earhart, Roosevelt wanted to obtain a pilot's license, although her husband rejected the idea. Earhart visited the White House fequently and supported the First Lady's efforts to improve the lives of working women. She also joined her campaign to promote world peace.

Courtesy of National Portrait Gallery, Smithsonian Institution NPG.82.135

Courtesy of the Franklin D. Roosevelt Presidential Library and Museum, Hyde Park, New York

Courtesy of the Eleanor Roosevelt National Historic Site, Val-Kill Hyde Park, New York

VISIT:

The Franklin D. Roosevelt Presidential Library and Museum
4079 Albany Post Rd.
Hyde Park, NY 12538

Eleanor Roosevelt National Historic Site
Val-Kill
Route 9G, Hyde Park, NY

The Home of Franklin Delano Roosevelt
Hyde Park, NY

fdrlibrary.org

ROSALYNN SMITH CARTER

Courtesy of The Carter Center

The Steel Magnolia Fights for Those in Need

On January 20, 1977 on Inauguration Day, Rosalynn Smith Carter walked hand in hand with her husband Jimmy, now the 39th President of the United States. The couple was from Plains, Georgia and paraded down Pennsylvania Avenue and into the White House. Not since Thomas Jefferson did any president, nevertheless a first lady, walk to the White House. Jimmy, as he liked to be called, was going to be a down-to-earth people's President. And Rosalynn had already told Americans what she planned to do.

As the first First Lady to ever make her own campaign promise, Rosalynn Carter would work to change laws to protect the mentally ill. She would pick up where she had left off as First Lady of Georgia.

Rosalynn had never forgotten the first time she met an individual with a developmental disability. That impression gave her purpose. She wanted to raise awareness that a mental disability should be treated the same as a physical disability, and that it is nothing to be ashamed of.

In her new position, Rosalynn couldn't wait to roll up her sleeves, get to work, and change the perception of mental illness.

Rosalynn went to Hollywood and spoke to producers, directors, and television and movie stars to encourage them to use sensitivity and accuracy when portraying people with a mental illness. She promoted public education programs to fight people's prejudices about the mentally ill. She also formed a commission that fought for insurance companies to cover mental illnesses. She fought for funds for research and prevention, and she encouraged more people to become mental health professionals. All of her efforts increased awareness of the issue of mental illness, and people's perceptions began to change.

The road to the White House was filled with many twists and turns. The couple married soon after their first date at the movies. As a young navy wife, Rosalynn followed Jimmy to six bases in seven years. She cooked, cleaned, took care of the bills, and learned how to make curtains, crochet and knit. She would knit argyle socks for her husband while she waited for him to come home on the weekends. On her sewing machine, she made clothes for herself and their baby. Their family would grow to include three sons, and later, a daughter named Amy.

Rosalynn grew up in a happy home with hardworking parents. Her mother sewed, and her father fixed automobiles and drove a school bus. He also served as town councilman. But Rosalynn's childhood ended, at age 12, when her father was diagnosed with leukemia. He died a year later in 1940.

As the eldest of four, this shy teenager proved her grit. Rosalynn took jobs to help pay the bills. Her mother had taught her how to sew, and Rosalynn helped her sew bridal gowns, suits, and dresses. She also became a hairdresser. Rosalynn said her mother "did what had to be done – she

President-Elect and Mrs. Carter and their daughter Amy on Inauguration Day, January 20, 1977

Library of Congress ppmsca.09758

As a teenager, Rosalynn helped her mother sew bridal gowns to help out at home with the finances after her father died. "You can do what you have to do," she said.

Because of her courage and southern roots, Rosalynn Carter was called a Steel Magnolia. The term Steel Magnolia symbolizes the strength of steel and the sensitivity of a flower.

On July 10, 2007, Rosalynn Carter testified before a U.S. House of Representatives subcommittee. She asked that mental illnesses, like physical illnesses, be covered by insurance.

Courtesy of The Carter Center

took charge." She said about herself, "I had to be strong…or appear to be strong."

Rosalynn graduated Valedictorian of her high school. Although her father had wanted more than than anything for her to get an education, she left Georgia Southwestern State University after two years because of financial reasons.

It is perhaps Rosalynn's disappointment at such a young age that made her a compassionate heart and a real fighter. This small-town girl who had read about faraway lands would help many people at home and abroad.

On Jimmy's campaign trail, she promised herself and the American people that she would be their voice. She was called a "Steel Magnolia" because she was courageous and fought for people who couldn't help themselves: the elderly, the caregivers, the homeless, the poor.

President Jimmy Carter knew that his childhood sweetheart and wife would not be content in the official hostess role. Rosalynn was his best friend, and he was the first to admit that she was his Chief Advisor. The two met every Wednesday for a meeting over lunch to discuss issues of the day. In addition to her work on trying to change the mental health laws, she urged Jimmy to appoint more women to senior level White House positions. Her office was in the East Wing, and she even held her own press conferences.

She did all of this while raising her daughter Amy who attended public school and loved to roller skate in the East Room of the White House and play with a Siamese cat named Misty Malarky Ying Yang. Amy's two older brothers with their families lived on the third floor. It was a full house! They ate on china from previous presidents, requested leftovers for their personal meals, and lowered the thermostat to conserve energy. They dressed simply too.

Rosalynn kept her campaign promise. She became active honorary chair of the President's Commission on Mental Health. This resulted in the passage of the Mental Health Systems Act of 1980. Each year she hosts the Rosalynn Carter Symposium on Mental Health.

She also kept her wedding vows. Jimmy and Rosalynn Carter are the longest married presidential couple in the history of the United States. They celebrated their 75th wedding anniversary in 2021, and besides helping others, they love to dance and watch movies. But her favorite thing to do is fly fishing.

Rosalynn Carter
Courtesy of The Carter Center

"Do what you can to show you care about other people, and you will make our world a better place."
~ Rosalynn Carter

President and Mrs. Carter
Courtesy of National Portrait Gallery, Smithsonian Institution, NPG.80.306 gift of Mr. and Mrs. James Earl Carter, Jr.

ROSALYNN SMITH CARTER
First Lady to 39th President (1977– 1981)

She was born Eleanor Rosalynn Smith on August 18, 1927 in Plains, Georgia to Wilburn Edgar Smith and Francis Allethea "Allie" Murray Smith. She never used her first name. She was not named after Eleanor Roosevelt, and yet she was her hero.

One month after Rosalynn's father died, her grandmother died. Her mother Allie cared for Rosalynn's grandfather and Rosalynn's siblings. Allie continued to work well into her 70s at a flower shop, even when Jimmy Carter became president. Her mother's life was a great influence upon her sensitivity to caregivers.

She married James Earl "Jimmy" Carter before her 19th birthday on July 7, 1946. He was a Naval Annapolis Academy graduate. She was a Methodist and then converted to Jimmy's faith, Baptist.

They had three sons: John William "Jack," James Earl "Chip," Donnel Jeffrey "Jeff," and then a daughter Amy Lynn in 1967. She studied literature and art at home while raising her children.

After Jimmy Carter's father died, the couple moved back to Plains, Georgia to manage the family's peanut farm. Rosalynn did the bookkeeping.

She became First Lady of Georgia in 1970. She put her sewing machine away because she did not have much time for making clothes. She wasn't one to buy fancy designer clothes. Reporters wrote about the sewing machine she brought to the White House.

Her Secret Service name was "Dancer."

Rosalynn began the first jazz festival and poetry festival at the White House. She commissioned an exhibition catalog, "American Crafts in the White House," for the Senate Ladies Luncheon on May 16, 1977.

Rosalynn Carter testified before a United States House of Representatives subcommittee on July 10, 2007, calling for mental illness to be covered on par with physical illness.

She served as Ambassador to Latin American countries and studied at home to learn Spanish. She made many political international missions. She visited a hospital and an orphanage tent of 30,000 Cambodian refugees in 1979. She was with President Carter during the peace talks negotiated with Israel and Egypt.

When President Carter ran for re-election in 1980, he had to stay in Washington D.C. because 52 Americans were being held hostage in Iran. Rosalynn went on the campaign trail for him, but Ronald Reagan won the election in 1981. Some would say that Rosalynn took

Mrs. Carter has worked for more than four decades to improve the quality of life for people with mental illnesses.

Co-founder of The Carter Center with former U.S. President Jimmy Carter, Mrs. Carter chairs the Center's Mental Health Task Force, an advisory body of experts, advocates, and consumers of mental health services that promotes positive change in the mental health field.

In recognition of her tireless fight for mental health and unwavering dedication to improving the lives of others, Rosalynn Carter was inducted into the National Women's Hall of Fame in 2001. She is one of four first ladies to earn that honor, including Abigail Adams, Eleanor Roosevelt and Hillary Clinton.

the loss much harder than Jimmy. She loves politics and she still had plenty of work to do!

She worked for the passage of the Equal Rights Amendment (ERA) and was unhappy when it failed to be ratified.

She helped to establish the Rosalynn Carter Institute for Caregiving (RCI) at Georgia Southwestern State University.

She co-launched "Every Child by Two," a nationwide campaign to publicize the need for early childhood immunization.

The Carter Center, founded in 1982 in Atlanta, Georgia, fights diseases around the world and promotes human rights.

The couple created the Rosalynn and Jimmy Carter Work Project, which is an annual week project for Habitat for Humanity. They helped build 4,000 houses around the world.

Rosalynn has been recognized with many honorary degrees and honors including: Volunteer of the Decade from the National Mental Health Association and the Presidential Medal of Freedom, America's highest civilian honor. "Time" magazine named her the second most powerful woman in the United States, and she tied with Mother Teresa for most admired.

Rosalynn Carter authored five books including her memoir, "First Lady from Plains."

She was elected a deacon at Maranatha Baptist Church in Plains, Georgia, 2006. She and Jimmy taught Sunday School. Many people traveled from all over the world to hear them preach and they like to take pictures with the couple after service.

In Seneca Falls, New York, in 2001, Rosalynn Carter was inducted into the National Women's Hall of Fame

Courtesy of The Carter Center

She also lobbied for the passage of an amendment to the Age Discrimination Act, raising the mandatory retirement age from 65 to 70.

The couple has been living in their four-bedroom ranch in Plains, Georgia, since 1961. They have 12 grandchildren and 10 great-grandchildren. Rosalynn remained devoted to humanitarian causes and continues to be the most active first lady in her post White House years. She also advocated for soldiers who returned from Afghanistan and Iran with post-traumatic stress disorder and depression.

She continues to speak on behalf of the mentally ill, senior citizens, the poor, and the homeless.

The Rosalynn Carter Butterfly Trail program has expanded internationally and helps increase habitats for Monarch Butterflies.

Even after she left the White House, Rosalynn Carter has continued her work fighting for those in need. Here she is giving hugs to a young girl in rural Ethiopia when she visited in 2007.

In 2018 in Atlanta, Georgia, she and her husband, former U.S. President Jimmy Carter, discuss some of the ways The Carter Center has been waging peace and fighting disease to build hope for millions around the world.

Images Courtesy of The Carter Center (pictured at right)

VISIT:

Carter Presidential Library and Museum
441 John Lewis Freedom Parkway NE
Atlanta, GA 30307

jimmycarterlibrary.gov

The Carter Center
One Copenhill
453 John Lewis Freedom Parkway NE
Atlanta, GA 30307

cartercenter.org

To learn more about Rosalynn Carter's causes:

rosalynncarter.org

habitat.org

rosalynncarterbutterflytrail.org

BARBARA PIERCE BUSH

Courtesy of the George H. W. Bush Presidential Library and Museum

Champion of Literacy

Mildred Kerr Bush couldn't stop wagging her tail with excitement when she published her book about the White House in 1992. Her dog mom, First Lady Barbara Bush, hoped many people would buy "Millie's Book" to benefit the Barbara Bush Foundation for Family Literacy, a charity that continues to give children books and helps them learn to read.

Millie, an English Springer Spaniel, wanted to follow in the paw prints of C. Fred Bush, who had been Mrs. Bush's Cocker Spaniel. Published in 1984, "C. Fred's Story: A Dog's Life" told tales about Barbara when she was second lady and her husband George Herbert Walker Bush was vice president during the Reagan administration.

Now that George was President and Millie could roam the White House, she could show off her knowledge of its history. Millie also knew everything about the Bush family too. That's a lot of people to keep track of! Barbara, nicknamed "Bar," had six children and twelve grandchildren.

Bar also championed the cause of literacy and traveled all over with Millie who appeared in many photographs with her.

"Millie's Book" is the first book written by a first lady as if it were written by Millie herself. Millie was named after Bar's friend Mildred Kerr. A Bush family tradition is to name children after family and good friends.

Millie, like Bar, had quite a sense of humor. In her book, she wrote about her pups, "They'd seen Rob Roy, Calvin Coolidge's famous white collie, in a portrait…not in the flesh….Dare I hope that Bar would consider having me in her portrait?"

To write a book from the dog's perspective was a way for Bar to get more people excited about reading, and to also learn about the history of the White House.

Mrs. Bush read to children in schools and at various organizations. She even read to kids on the set of Sesame Street.

"Hello, it's nice to see you again, Big Bird," said Mrs. Bush.

"Oh, it's nice to see you too," said Big Bird. "Mrs. Bush is here today to read us a book that I

"Treat everyone equally, don't look down on anyone, use your voices for good, read all the great books."

~ Barbara Bush

Barbara Bush reads Dr. Seuss' "Horton Hatches the Egg," to Rock Prairie Elementary School children at the George Bush Presidential Library, 2002.

Courtesy of the George H. W. Bush Presidential Library and Museum

Images Courtesy of the George H.W. Bush Presidential Library and Museum

In New York in October 1989, Mrs. Bush read to Big Bird and children on Sesame Street.

Barbara Bush works at her desk at Walker's Point, Kennebunkport, Maine, August 22, 1990.

borrowed from the Sesame Street Library. It's called Peter's Chair by Ezra Jack Keats."

As Mrs. Bush read to the children, Count Dracula counted 15 storybook pages!

Another talk show host, Oprah Winfrey, interviewed Mrs. Bush in 1989. "I love my life. I can't wait to get up in the morning. That's pretty lucky," Mrs. Bush told Oprah.

Dressed in her "Barbara Blue" outfits with her signature triple pearl necklace, she became beloved by many and lived life in the traditional role as a wife and a mother. Barbara met George Bush at the age of 16 at a Christmas dance in 1941, and they married five years later. She followed her husband, the youngest Navy pilot, around the country, from base to base, and grew their family. Somewhere along the way with the rise of the women's movement, Bar started to doubt her decision to not have a career of her own. But that didn't last too long.

She found her passion outside the important role of motherhood, too, and that was literacy. She believed that literacy was the answer to solving some of society's problems including poverty, homelessness, and even AIDS.

As the daughter of a publisher, reading was always an integral part of her life. Her father was President of McCall Corporation, which published popular women's magazines. She remembered growing up in a home with all her family gathered together and reading at night.

Later her son Neil would be diagnosed as dyslexic. Some say this is when she became interested in literacy, but she stated it is because she believed literacy could help everyone lead better lives and solve some of society's problems.

Since her foundation's inception in 1989, millions of people across the 50 states have been affected.

On April 17, 2018, Barbara Bush passed away at their family's home on the ranch in Houston, Texas. George H.W. Bush, known for his socks, wore a pair covered in books to honor his wife's commitment to family literacy which raised more than $110 million dollars.

Not too long after, on November 30, 2018, he died. President Bush's service dog, a yellow Labrador named Sully, stayed by his casket.

The "Today" show interviewed granddaughters, twins Jenna Hager Bush and namesake, Barbara Bush. Jenna, who works on the show as a host, recalled her young daughter Mila's wise words, "Gampy had to get to Grammy so they could decorate their Christmas tree."

"They had never spent a Christmas apart in their 73 years," said Jenna. Jenna now has her own popular book club on the "Today" show.

In her memory, every year The Barbara Bush Foundation for Family Literacy hosts a benefit called a "Celebration of Reading."

Mrs. Bush reads to children in the White House Library on July 24, 1990.

Courtesy of the George H.W. Bush Presidential Library and Museum

Barbara Bush also loved to needlepoint. Her needlepoint rug, shown here in the residence of the White House, took eight years to make. She began it in China in 1975 and finished in 1983, 17 countries and 36 states later. She stitched her grandchildren's initials and important dates. She said, "I wanted something that I wouldn't outgrow, something that would last forever." Right, seated far left, she is showing her work to friends in March 1978.

Images Courtesy of the George H.W. Bush Presidential Library and Museum

Barbara Pierce Bush
Courtesy of the George H.W. Bush Presidential Library and Museum

BARBARA PIERCE BUSH
First Lady to 41st President (1989 – 1993)
Second Lady to 40th Vice President (1981 – 1989)
Mother of 43rd President (2001 – 2009)

    Barbara Pierce Bush was born on June 8, 1925 in New York City to Marvin Pierce and Pauline Robinson Pierce. Her father was President of McCall Publishing Corporation. Her mother died in a car accident when Barbara was pregnant with her second child, Robin. Her father later remarried. Barbara was the third child with one sister and two brothers.

    She attended Milton Public School and Rye Country Day School and a boarding school named Ashley Hall in South Carolina. While a freshman at Smith College in Massachusetts, she was captain of the soccer team. She attended for one year and then married George H. W. Bush at 19 on January 6, 1945 at First Presbyterian Church in Rye, New York He became a millionaire by the age of 30 in the oil industry and set out to serve his country.

    He was a Navy lieutenant pilot when they married, and they had six children: George Walker, Pauline Robinson "Robin," John Ellis "Jeb" Bush, Neil Mallon, Marvin Pierce, and Dorothy "Doro."

    Because of her grandmotherly ways and quick wit, First Lady Barbara Bush became popular. She always focused her attention on family, faith and friends. She could also be tough. Her children called her style a "benevolent dictatorship." The Secret Service nicknamed her the "Enforcer."

    She made history like Abigail Adams when her son George Walker became the 43rd President of the United States. Unlike Abigail, she was alive to see his inauguration. Her daughter-in-law, First Lady Laura Bush, was a librarian.

    Jeb Bush was the 43rd Governor of Florida and made a run for the presidency in 2016. Neil and Marvin are businessmen. Doro is an author and philanthropist. Barbara and George had 12 grandchildren.

    Her husband called for a "kinder, gentler nation." They were filled with compassion because they had known deep sadness. Their three-year-old daughter, Robin, had died from leukemia. The shock and grief turned Barbara's hair white prematurely, and from that moment on she opened her heart to care for everyone.

    During the summers, the Bush family enjoyed their home in Kennebunkport, Maine. They added another dog to their home, Ranger, one of Millie's pups.

    In 2013, Neil and Maria Bush founded the Barbara Bush Houston Literacy Foundation.

George and Barbara Bush married on January 6, 1945. The couple is buried on the grounds of the George H.W. Bush Presidential Site in Texas, alongside daughter Robin.
Courtesy of the George H.W. Bush Presidential Library and Museum

When George W. Bush became president, twins Jenna and Barbara moved into the White House, and their grandmother visited them often. President George Walker Bush had a beloved dog, too, and that was Barney, whom was known as "First Dog."

During his career as a navy pilot, the Bushes moved approximately 29 times. They settled in Texas in 1959. George Bush was elected Republican Party Chairman three years later, and she became active in women's organizations and clubs.

Barbara became Second Lady of the United States in 1981. George Bush was Vice President to Ronald Reagan for two terms.

On George's Inauguration Day, the Bushes walked part of the parade route back to the White House like the Carters. They also held an open house Inaugural Reception like the Tafts.

Barbara Bush was the first First Lady to hire an African American as her press secretary. She was committed to civil rights and attended many Martin Luther King Day programs at local schools.

She made headlines when she visited Grandma's House, a pediatric AIDS care center.

She was the first First Lady to throw the opening pitch at a baseball game. That was the first game for the Texas Rangers owned by her son, George W.

Barbara Bush developed Graves disease while in the White House. She and President George H. W. Bush believed in volunteerism. He created a program called 1,000 Points of Light. In addition to literacy, Barbara Bush served as AmeriCares ambassador-at-large, and on the board of the Mayo-Clinic. She supported a variety of organizations including the Leukemia Society, Ronald McDonald House and the Boys and Girls Club of America.

The family enjoyed summers at Kennebunkport, Maine and life, after the presidency at the ranch in Texas.

She kept a journal and published books including: "Barbara Bush: A Memoir," "Barbara Bush: Reflections," and "First Mom: Wit and Wisdom of Barbara Bush." Her historic speech, "Your Own True Colors," was delivered to the 1990 graduating class at Wellesley.

Faith was important to her and she was Episcopalian. She died on April 17, 2018. Both she and George had state funerals. The couple is buried, along with daughter Robin, on the grounds of the George H. Bush Presidential Library in College Station, Texas.

VISIT:

**George H.W. Bush Presidential Library & Museum
1000 George Bush Dr. W
College Station, TX 77845**

bush41.org

Visit

barbarabush.org

Courtesy of the George H.W. Bush Presidential Library and Museum

Afterword

I was almost at my halfway mark when I was writing about Edith Roosevelt. She had once lived at Sagamore Hill, the Summer White House, only about 30 minutes away from my own home. I had only visited once, and that was when I was in the 5th grade. My memory, though very good, was fuzzy. I recalled Theodore's animals mounted on the wall from his safaris, but Edith…hmmmmm. Edith, I couldn't remember her presence in the house. Perhaps it was because my focus was on the president. That's what we learned about when I was in elementary school. Not much attention was paid to the first ladies.

So on a hot day in June in 2019, my husband and I drove on the Long Island Expressway early in the morning to Sagamore Hill in Oyster Bay. The view is gorgeous with homes high on hills and boats on the bay.

At the home on this grand estate of grassy hills and apple orchards, we saw a tall copper-beech tree without branches. Its trunk would be cut down soon, too. Theodore Roosevelt had planted this tree himself 125 years ago. Now they were planning to make souvenirs from the wood. Oh, the stories that dying tree could tell.

I sat on the piazza in a rocking chair and overlooked the grounds. The view is different now, as the trees block the bay which the Roosevelts once enjoyed. Many summers ago, Edith had knitted on that piazza and reminisced about her life. I was trying to imagine her living there with her six kids and Theodore coming home with his Safari trophies, book in hand and asking the cook for his favorite fried chicken in white gravy.

The curator let us in, and I recalled the dark paneling and all the animal heads mounted on the walls.

And there, to my left, was Edith's drawing room. I had no recollection.

I saw four windows draped with blue curtains in lace. The shelves packed with her books. The desk where she wrote the checks. The sofas where she entertained her guests, the ones she wouldn't let her husband and his friends sit on.

The kitchen, so very hot in summertime, where the cook made meals for the family. The maroon-rimmed china in Edith's cabinet, most likely a wedding present. The dining room where Henry Ford, Thomas Edison and Woodrow Wilson joined them for a meal and in conversation. Theodore expected his children to be able to ask them questions, too.

The piano and mandolin in the living area played by the children, and that German book of fairy tales that Theodore translated to them.

We traveled through the home, up the stairs, to the bedrooms.

Our guide showed us Alice's bedroom, Edith's bedroom, the boys' bedroom with the Harvard banner, and the rooms for the governess and servants, nanny, seamstress, and cook. In the hallway, a Thomas Nast drawing of Santa Claus and stockings with all the names of the children.

The guest room where many stayed including Eleanor Roosevelt. The quilt on its bed, a gift, embroidered with every name of everyone who slept in that room.

Edith's well-traveled trunks with her name on it, the linens with her initials embroidered on them, the mirror on her dresser where she caught her image. Her portrait on the wall, and the one she didn't like with its background in blue on the backside of it, hidden from public view.

Afterwards, I had the pleasure of speaking with a curator by the name of Elizabeth "Betsy" DeMaria who generously gave of her time and agreed to share with me some of the photos you see in this book.

We walked the path they once walked. We then drove a few minutes down the road to Young Cemetery and visited the gravesites of Theodore and Edith Roosevelt. Only a short while before, we saw the beds where they each had died.

That's when I was really moved.

History shouldn't only be about dates and facts. It's really stories about people who once lived real lives. It's the same as hearing stories about people in your own families. No matter what period of the time they lived in, they experienced moments in life that we all do, from its sorrows to its joys.

We learn from the past. When we can make the past come alive again, we better understand our present. This helps us to face our future. It gives us perspective.

Whenever and if ever you have a chance to visit a historical property, go. Do it. Take it all in. Soak it up! In doing so, you will learn more about yourself, what you want to contribute, and who you want to become.

That's what happened to me.

~ Debra Scala Giokas

"What about the second ladies?"

A month later, while on vacation in Rehoboth, Delaware, at Browseabout Books on July 3, 2019, my husband and I had the pleasure of meeting then former Second Lady of the United States, Dr. Jill Biden. She signed her book, "Where the Light Enters: Building a Family, Discovering Myself." I mentioned my project. She replied, "What about the second ladies?" Then she told me something else. Dr. Jill Biden, wife of the 46th President of the United States and the first First Lady to hold a paying job while in the White House, needlepoints.

First Lady Trivia

Below are quotes from some of the first ladies you read about here.
Do you know who said what?

1. "I thanked the happy fate that had given me a summer wedding day because I needed all outdoors for the kind of party I wanted to give."

2. "It is one of my sources of happiness never to desire a knowledge of other people's business."

3. "Under all circumstances, we must never desert ourselves."

4. "Crossing the uplands of time, Skirting the borders of night, Scaling the face of the peak of dreams, We enter the region of light, And hastening on with eager intent, Arrive at the rainbow's end, And here uncover the pot of gold Buried deep in the heart of a friend." *(hint: It's a poem.)*

5. "Never lose sight of the fact that the most important yardstick of your success will be how you treat other people – your family, friends, co-workers, and even strangers you meet along the way."

6. "I taught him to form the letters, but he was an apt scholar, and acquired all the rest of it for himself."

7. "I am determined to be cheerful and happy in whatever situation I may find myself. For I have learned that the greater part of our misery or unhappiness is determined not by our circumstance but by our disposition."

8. "I will stand by you – not for duty, not for pity, not for honour – but for love – trusting, protecting, comprehending love."

9. "I know what's best for the president. I put him in the White House. He does well when he listens to me and poorly when he does not."

10. "Great difficulties may be surmounted by patience and perseverance."

11. "The independent girl is truly of quite modern origin, and usually is a most bewitching little piece of humanity."

12. "Great minds discuss ideas; average minds discuss events; small minds discuss people."

13. "Do what you can to show you care about other people, and you will make our world a better place."

14. "I think imagination is one of the greatest blessings of life."

1. Helen Taft 2. Dolley Madison 3. Louisa Adams 4. Grace Coolidge 5. Barbara Bush 6. Eliza Johnson 7. Martha Washington 8. Edith Wilson 9. Florence Harding 10. Abigail Adams 11. Lou Henry Hoover 12. Eleanor Roosevelt 13. Rosalynn Carter 14. Edith Roosevelt

First Ladies of the United States

Are you hooked on the history of the first ladies of the United States? Not all women who have served as a first lady were spouses to the presidents. If the president was a bachelor or a widower or if his wife could not perform the role, other female relatives fufilled the duties. Here is a chronological list to help you on your own learning journey:

Martha Washington
Abigail Adams
Martha "Patsy" Jefferson Randolph
(daughter to President Thomas Jefferson)
Dolley Madison
Elizabeth Monroe
Louisa Adams
Emily Donelson
(niece to President Andrew Jackson)
Angelica Van Buren
(daughter-in-law to President Andrew Jackson)
Anna Harrison
Letitia Tyler *(wife to President John Tyler)*
Julia Tyler *(second wife)*
Sarah Childress Polk
Margaret "Peggy" Taylor
Abigail Fillmore
Jane Pierce
Harriet Lane
(niece to President Buchanan)
Mary Lincoln
Eliza Johnson
Julia Grant
Lucy Hayes
Lucretia Garfield
Ellen Arthur*

Frances Cleveland
Caroline Harrison
Frances Cleveland
Ida McKinley
Edith Roosevelt
Helen Taft
Ellen Wilson *(wife to Woodrow Wilson)*
Edith Bolling Galt Wilson *(second wife)*
Florence Harding
Grace Coolidge
Lou Hoover
Eleanor Roosevelt
Bess Truman
Mamie Eisenhower
Jacqueline Kennedy
Lady Bird Johnson
Patricia Nixon
Betty Ford
Rosalynn Carter
Nancy Reagan
Barbara Bush
Hillary Clinton
Laura Bush
Michelle Obama
Melania Trump
Dr. Jill Biden

*She died before President Chester Arthur took office and he did not officially give anyone the title. His sister, Mary Arthur McElroy, performed the duties of first lady.

First Ladies and the Tradition of the White House Christmas Tree

Lou Henry Hoover supervised the decoration of the White House Christmas tree in 1929. That began the tradition of putting the first lady in charge.

1889. **President Benjamin Harrison** was the first president to have displayed a Christmas tree in the White House in 1889. The tree was in the Yellow Oval Room on the second floor, which was the library. Before 1891 there was no electricity in the White House, so they used wax candles. In **1934**, **President Franklin Delano Roosevelt** used candles on the East Hall's tree to return to the tradition.

1895. **President Grover Cleveland** lit the tree with red, white and blue bulbs.

1912. While **President Howard Taft and Nellie** were in Panama, their children set up a tree in the Blue Room because their seven cousins were visiting.

1929. After **Lou Henry Hoover** began the tradition for first ladies to decorate the tree, decades later **Jacqueline Kennedy** began the tradition of having a theme.

1961. **Jacqueline Kennedy** decorated with characters from the ballet, "Nutcracker Suite."

Courtesy of Benjamin Harrison Presidential Site
The front parlor of the Benjamin Harrison Home at the Presidential Site in Indianapolis, Indiana, features a large tree similar to the one decorated for his grandchildren in 1889 in the White House. Authentic decorations such as wooden soldiers, cotton batting ornaments, hand-blown glass figures, and candles adorn this tree.

1964. For her "Early American" theme, **Lady Bird Johnson** selected gingerbread men.

1969. **Pat Nixon** commissioned disabled workers to make the flowers of each state for her theme of "Flowers of America."

1974. To celebrate "American Crafts," **Betty Ford** commissioned women in Appalachia and senior citizen groups to make patchwork ornaments. For America's Bicentennial in **1976**, the theme was "America is Love." Red, white, and blue were in the color scheme from the tree to the rest of the White House decorations.

1978. **Rosalynn Carter's** theme, "Antique Toys," consisted of Victorian dolls and miniature furniture from Margaret Woodbury Strong Museum in Rochester, New York. **President Jimmy Carter** was the first president to recognize Hanukkah with a menorah lighting in **1979**.

1986. **Nancy Reagan** chose "Mother Goose" nursery rhymes from "Little Jack Horner" to "Mary Had A Little Lamb" to "The Little Old Lady Who Lives In A Shoe." For her two terms as first lady to be consistent with her "Just Say No" to drugs campaign, patients at a drug rehab program called Second Genesis made the ornaments.

1991. For "Needlework," **Barbara Bush** decorated the Blue Room tree with 1,200 needlepoint ornaments, three of which she herself made by hand. Her "Saintly Stitchers" of St. Martin's Episcopal Church in Houston, Texas made a needlepoint village and figurines for a Noah's Ark, built by White House staff carpenters. She said that many men also did the needlepoint, some who had never done the craft before. It took a total of 125,000 needlepointing hours to complete the project.

1994. **Hillary Clinton**

celebrated the "Twelve Days of Christmas," as interpreted by art students around the country. She and her husband, President Bill Clinton, sang the song with children.

2002. **Laura Bush's** "All

Creatures Great And Small," celebrated the important role that animals play in the White House. The tree, which had a red color theme, featured ornaments designed by an artist from each state, based on a native bird. In **2005**, she chose "All Things Bright and Beautiful," and her trees glistened with white lilies and crystal spheres wrapped in iridescent garland.

2009. In her first White House

Christmas, **Michelle Obama's** theme was "Reflect, Rejoice and Renew." She sent 800 leftover ornaments to community groups, and asked each group to create their favorite for "United States Landmarks." In **2016** for "Gift of the Holidays," there were larger-than-life yarn replicas of the Obamas' dogs Sunny and Bo.

2017. **Melania Trump** chose

"Time-Honored Traditions," and the 53 trees filled with 12,000 ornaments paid respect to 200 years of holiday traditions at the White House. In **2018,** she selected 40 red trees and hung 14,000 red ornaments elsewhere in the White House as "a symbol of valor and bravery."

2021. **Dr. Jill Biden** chose

"Gifts from the Heart." The theme, said to be inspired by people the Bidens met as they traveled the country that year in the midst of a pandemic, focused

Courtesy of George H.W. Bush Presidential Library and Museum

One of the Christmas trees in the White House, 1991. Barbara Bush's theme was needlework.

on faith, family, and friendship; a love of the arts, learning, and nature; gratitude, service, and community; unity and peace. Dr. Biden hung six stockings for her grandchildren, and in each one placed an orange which is a family tradition dating back to her grandmother. During the Great Depression when food was hard to come by, oranges were a treat.

More Fun Facts!

The 42nd Second Lady Joan Adams Mondale, a potter and an art historian, and wife of **Vice President Walter Mondale**, used her platform to promote the positive impact of crafts in the United States. Beginning in 1977, she decorated the Vice-President's Mansion with "Creativity Trees," to celebrate the "vitality and creativity of the American imagination." American crafters and artisans made the ornaments. Unfortunately, the tradition did not last, but the White House trees over the years have called upon and continue to call upon the creativity of Americans.

President George H.W. Bush proclaimed 1993 as the "Year of the American Craft: A Celebration of the Creative Work of the Hand."

Every year the White House Historical Association commemorates the legacy of a president through its ornament program. **First Lady Jacqueline Kennedy** founded the Association in 1961. In 2021, the official ornament remembered the presidency of Lyndon Baines Johnson. The public may purchase these ornaments.

Acknowledgments

I became who I am because of the help of so many others. Thank you to…

My husband, George, who believes in me and in this project and read and edited everything, and cooked dinners so I could get this finished. (Martha and Barbara and I have good taste in men's names!) You are my heart.

My parents who gave me a loving home, encouragement and took me to the library, and my brother and sister for their support.

My grandparents, including my Grandpa Marty, who said, "So you want to be a writer?" And he was more than fine with that. And Grandma Lois for the crochet lessons.

My two college professors from Stony Brook University who have passed on, yet their influence never will: Professor Hugh G. Cleland and Professor Diane Fortuna.

My first teacher, Kathleen Fitzgibbons Weinman, whom I had the good fortune to reconnect with 49 years later and who read the first draft of every one of these stories.

Joe Perry, for editorial assistance and for challenging me.

My illustrator and friend, the talented Mary Ryan Reeves, for the cover art.

And my beloved dogs Bella and now Zoe Ana who kept me company throughout this long process.

I also want to thank the keepers of our nation's treasures. They are the librarians, curators and historians who perserve and tell our country's stories and do a fine job at that. They make learning history, fun. Thank you to the following for your kindness and generosity of spirit in sharing your knowledge and your images: **Michelle Gullion,** Archives Director & Curator, First Ladies' National Historic Site; **Dawn Bonner,** Manager of Visual Resources, Mount Vernon Ladies' Association; **Kelly Cobble,** Curator, Adams National Historical Park; **Hannah Elder,** Assistant Librarian for Rights and Reproductions, Massachusetts Historical Society; **Lisa Kathleen Graddy,** Curator, Division of Political History, National Museum of American History Smithsonian Institution; **Bethany W. Sullivan,** Director, James Madison Museum of Orange County Heritage; **Hilarie M. Hicks,** Senior Research Historian and **Jenniffer Powers,** Collections Manager, James Madison's Montpelier; **Susan Joyce Webster,** Registrar and Curator, and **Elise Allison,** Archivist, Greensboro History Museum; **Kathy Frost,** Curator, Aurora Historical Society, Millard Fillmore Presidential Site; **Kendra Hinkle,** Museum Specialist, Cultural Resource Manager, Andrew Johnson National Historic Site; **the late Mark D. Evans,** Collector, Avon, NY and one of the founders of the Buffalo History Museum; **Elizabeth (Betsy) DeMaria,** former Museum Technician/Archivist, and **Lindsay Davenport**, Museum Technician, Sagamore Hill National Historic Site; **Ruth Horstman,** Education Technician, **Robb Mair,** Administrative Assistant, William Howard Taft National Historic Site; **Farron Smith,** Founder, and **Morgan Herbert,** Executive Director, Edith Bolling Wilson Birthplace Museum; **Mark Peterson** and **Asantewa Boakyewa,** Senior Manager of Interpretation & Collections, Woodrow Wilson House National Trust for Historic Preservation; **Penny White,** Reference Librarian, University of Virginia; **Sherry Hall,** Director, Harding Home Presidential Site; **Professor Katherine A. S. Sibley,** Saint Joseph's University; **Jen Cabiya,** Digital Projects Coordinator, Ohio History Connection; **Victoria Highs,** Museum & Education Manager and **Paul Carnahan,** Librarian, and **Marjorie Strong,** Vermont Historical Society; **Karen Maxville,** Registrar and **Craig Wright,** Supervisory Archivist, Herbert Hoover Presidential Library; **Paul Sparrow,** Director, **Patrick Fahey,** Archives Technician, **Matthew C. Hanson,** Photo Archivist, and **Michelle M. Frauenberger,** Museum Collections Manager/Registrar, Franklin D. Roosevelt Presidential Library and Museum; **Michael Autenrieth,** Park Ranger, Eleanor Roosevelt National Historic Site; **Mary Finch,** AV/Archivist, **Elizabeth Staats,** Archivist and **Mark Wallace,** Digital Imaging Technician, George H.W. Bush Presidential Library National Archives and Records Administration; **Youlanda Logan,** Archivist, Jimmy Carter Library; **Melissa Montgomery,** Special Assistant to Rosalynn Carter; **Deanna Congileo,** Vice President of Communications (retired), The Carter Center; **Jennifer E. Capps,** Vice President of Curatorship and Exhibition, Benjamin Harrison Presidential Site; the **Library of Congress,** the **Smithsonian Institution Open Access** program; and all of the helpful librarians in my own hometown at the **Sayville Library,** especially the Children's Librarian, **Miss Michelle.**

Bibliography

BOOKS

Allgor, C. (2006) *A Perfect Union: Dolley Madison and the Creation of the American Nation.* Henry Holt and Company.

Anthony, C. (2013) *Ida McKinley: The Turn of the Century First Lady through War, Assassination, and Secret Disability.* Kent State University Press, Published in cooperation with The National First Ladies Library.

Boller, Jr., P. (1988) *Presidential Wives: An Anecdotal History.* Oxford University Press.

Bleyer, B. (2016) *Sagamore Hill: Theodore Roosevelt's Summer White House.* History Press.

Bush, B. (1990) *Millie's Book, As Dictated to Barbara Bush.* William Morrow and Company.

Carter, R. (1984) *First Lady From Plains.* Fawcett, Gold Medal.

Cook, W. (2019) *Memories of the White House.* Originally published 1911, Middletown, DE.

Cooper, I. (2018) *Eleanor Roosevelt: Fighter for Justice.* Abrams Books for Young Readers.

Gormley, B. (1997) *First Ladies: Women Who Called The White House Home.* Scholastic.

Gould, L., ed. (2001) *American First Ladies: Their Lives and Their Legacy*, Second Edition. Routledge.

Harris, B. (revised by Ross, L.) (2011) *First Ladies Fact Book.* Black Dog & Levanthal Publishers.

Holton, W. (2009) *Abigail Adams.* Free Press, A Division of Simon and Schuster.

Krull, K. (2017) *America's First Ladies.* HarperCollins.

Lambert, D. *The Undying Past of Shenandoah National Park.* Roberts Rinehart, Inc. Publishers in cooperation with Shenandoah Natural History Association

Marton, K. (2001) *Hidden Power: Presidential Marriages That Shaped Our Recent History.* Pantheon Books.

Mayer, D. (2004) *Lou Henry Hoover: A Prototype for First Ladies.* Nova History Publications.

Mayo, E., ed, (1996) *The Smithsonian Book of First Ladies.* Henry Holt and Company.

Morris, S. (2001) *Edith Kermit Roosevelt: Portrait of a First Lady.* Modern Library.

McCullough, N. (2008) *First Kids: True Stories of All Presidents' Children.* Scholastic.

Page, S. (2019) *The Matriarch, Barbara Bush and the Making of an American Dynasty.* Twelve, Hachette Book Group.

Pastan, A. (2001) *First Ladies: Meet forty-four dynamic women from Martha Washington to Laura Bush.* DK Eyewitness Books, In Association with the Smithsonian Institution, Dorling Kindersley Publishing.

Santella, A. (2002) *U.S. Presidential Inaugurations: Cornerstones of Freedom*, Children's Press, a Division of Scholastic, Inc.

Sawyer, K. (2006) *Eleanor Roosevelt*, DK Publishing.

Sferrazza, C. (2000) *America's First Families.* Simon & Schuster.

Simon, C. (2000) *Encyclopedia of First Ladies*. Grolier Publishing.

Slade, S. (2008) *Martha Washington, First Lady of the United States*, Picture Window Books.

Souter, G. and J. (2009) *Millard Fillmore Our Thirteenth President*. The Child's World.

Taft, H. (2014) *Recollections of Full Years*. Big Byte Books.

Thacker-Estrada, E. (2001) *The Heart of the Fillmore Presidency: Abigail Powers Fillmore and the White House Library*, White House Studies, Nova Science Publishers.

Thomas, L. (2016) *Louisa: The Extraordinary Life of Mrs. Adams*. Penguin Publishing Group.

Twain, M., Amith, E. ed., (2010) *Autobiography of Mark Twain*. Volume I. University of California Press.

Willets, G. (1908) *Inside History of the White House*, originally published by Christian Herald.

Williams, F. (2014) *The Bride of The White House: The Marriage of President Grover Cleveland to Frances Folsom*, 1886, Big Byte Books.

ARTICLES and BLOG POSTS

Ackerman, S. J. (July 4, 2014) The first celebrity first lady: Frances Cleveland. *The Washington Post*.

Anthony, C. (September 1, 2016) The Unusual & Rare Examples of Ida McKinley's Handwriting. firstladies.org.

Anthony, C. (July 2, 2015) Ida McKinley: Not the Historical Figure But the Person. firstladies.org.

Anthony, C. (July 1, 2013) The New Home of an Old President. firstladies.org.

Butler, B. Ida Saxton McKinley Had a Penchant for Aqua, Standing Collars, Tucked Chiffon, Lace, Velvet Ribbon, Paillettes…and Monkey Fur. beesfirstappearance.wordpress.com

Butler, B. (November/December 2013) First Lady Ida Saxton McKinley and her Crocheted Slippers. *Piecework*.

Conroy, S. (May 8, 2000) Frank and Grover: A Love Story. *The Washington Post*.

Eschner, K. (August 15, 2017) Florence Harding, Not Eleanor Roosevelt, May Have Created the Modern First Lady. *Smithsonian Magazine*

Evans, M. (Spring 2010) Buffalo's Own First Lady: Frances Folsom Cleveland. *Western New York Heritage*, 13 (1).

Finn, N. (December 1, 2018) How a Christmas Dance Led to a Dynasty. eonline.com

Gleeson, J. (September 19, 2019) The White House Christmas Tree Tradition Goes Back Farther Than You Might Think. *Country Living*

Hagan, D. (May-June 2012). The Old House. *New England Home*.

Heller, D. February 20, 2012) Craft in the White House. craftcouncil.org.

Hyde, N. (January 30, 1977) Rosalynn Carter's Fashion. *The Washington Post*.

Kahn, E. (June 19, 2014) What's a Tiara Like You Doing on Reality TV? *New York Times*.

Kamm, H. (November 10, 1979) Mrs. Carter Visits Thai Camp: It's Like Nothing I've Seen. *The New York Times*.

Kennedy, Robert C. Blessed be the Union: On this Day, *The New York Times*, 2001

Knibbs, K. (November 22, 2017) The Raccoon Who Moved Into the White House on Thanksgiving. theringer.com

Mayer, B. (July 1, 1989) First Lady Stimulates New Interest in Hand-Stitched Home Accessories. *The Boston Globe*.

McCaslin, J. (July 21, 2018) Discovering Hoover and his hidden jewel in Shenandoah National Park. *RappNews*.

Nunnery, J. (January 30, 2018) George and Martha Washington: The Many Sides of Love. *The House and Home Magazine*.

Oosterhuis, K. (December 15, 2011) Crafts of Christmas Past: Mondale Creativity Trees. craftcouncil.org.

Pietrusza, D. Wombats and Such: Calvin and Grace Coolidge and Their Pets. davidpietrusza.com

Smart, P. (May 2, 2012) Eleanor Roosevelt Knit-In in Hyde Park on May 6. *Hudson Valley One*.

Spencer, H. (JUne 13, 2008) The President's Mountain School, hoover.gov.

Svrluga, S. (April 28, 2015) After George Washington dies, his wife burned his letters, Except these. *The Washington Post*.

Valjak, D. (April 23, 2018) An alligator, a cursing parrot, a pair of white mice, a badger and opossums - the weirdest pets of U.S. presidents. *The Vintage News*.

Vejnoska, J. (August 12, 2017) Rosalynn Carter ready to add to great life with 90th birthday. *The Atlanta Journal-Constitution*.

Tribune Content Agency. (July 18, 2014) Exhibit to honor Buffalo's First Lady, Frances Folsom Cleveland.

(November 24, 1941) How to Knit. *LIFE Magazine*.

(September 21, 1941) 'Knit for Defense' Tea: Event Here to Start to Organize Women of Nation. *The New York Times*.

(September 28, 1941) Mass Knitting Movement To Be Launched Tuesday. *The New York Times*.

(October 1, 1941) Mrs. Roosevelt Urges All Women To Knit for Soldiers and Sailors. *The New York Times*.

(May 13, 2021) The Mexican-American war in a nutshell. *Constitution Daily*.

(May 29, 1886) The White House Bride. *The New York Times*.

PAMPHLETS

Ryan, F. (1950) Centennial of the White House Library. Information from Fillmore House Guides' Book.

Books in the First White House Library, compliments of the Aurora Historical Society.

WEBSITES

abigailadamsbirthplace.com
americanheritage.com
aurorahistoricalsociety.com
www.americanhistory.si.edu
barbarabush.org
biography.com
britannica.com
buffalohistory.org
bush41.org
cartercenter.org
centerforknitandcrochet.org
constitutioncenter.org
coolidgefoundation.org
criticalpast.com
dolleymadisonpapers.org
edithbollingwilson.org
fdrlibrary.org
firstladies.org
firstladies.c-span.org
forbeslibrary.org
founders.archives.gov
habitat.org
hardingpresidentialsites.org
history.com
historylink.org
hoover.org
interweave.com
jimmycarterlibrary.gov

knitty.com
library.harvard.edu
loc.gov
masshist.org
millercenter.org
montpelier.org
mountvernon.org
nps.gov
nyhistory.org
obamawhitehouse.archives.gov
ohiomemory.org
ourwhitehouse.org
pbs.org
presidentcleveland.org
presidentialpetmuseum.com
rosalynncarter.org
rosalynncarterbutterflytrail.org
si.edu
si.edu/openaccess
smithsonianmag.com
thejamesmadisonmuseum.net
theodorerooseveltcenter.org
vermonthistory.org
whitehouse.gov
whitehousehistory.org
woodrowwilson.org
woodrowwilsonhouse.org
womenshistory.org

ABOUT THE AUTHOR

Debra Scala Giokas is a
marketing communications professional.
A member of the Society of Children's Book Writers
and Illustrators, she is the author of a picture book
about American fashion designer, Claire McCardell.
It's entitled, "Claire: The Little Girl Who Climbed to the Top
and Changed the Way Women Dress."
The companion coloring book is "Claire's Closet."
An avid crocheter herself, Debra is a
professional member of the Crochet Guild of America.
She lives on Long Island in New York
with her husband and their two dogs.
She speaks at libraries, historical societies and
museums. For more information,
visit debrascalagiokas.com.

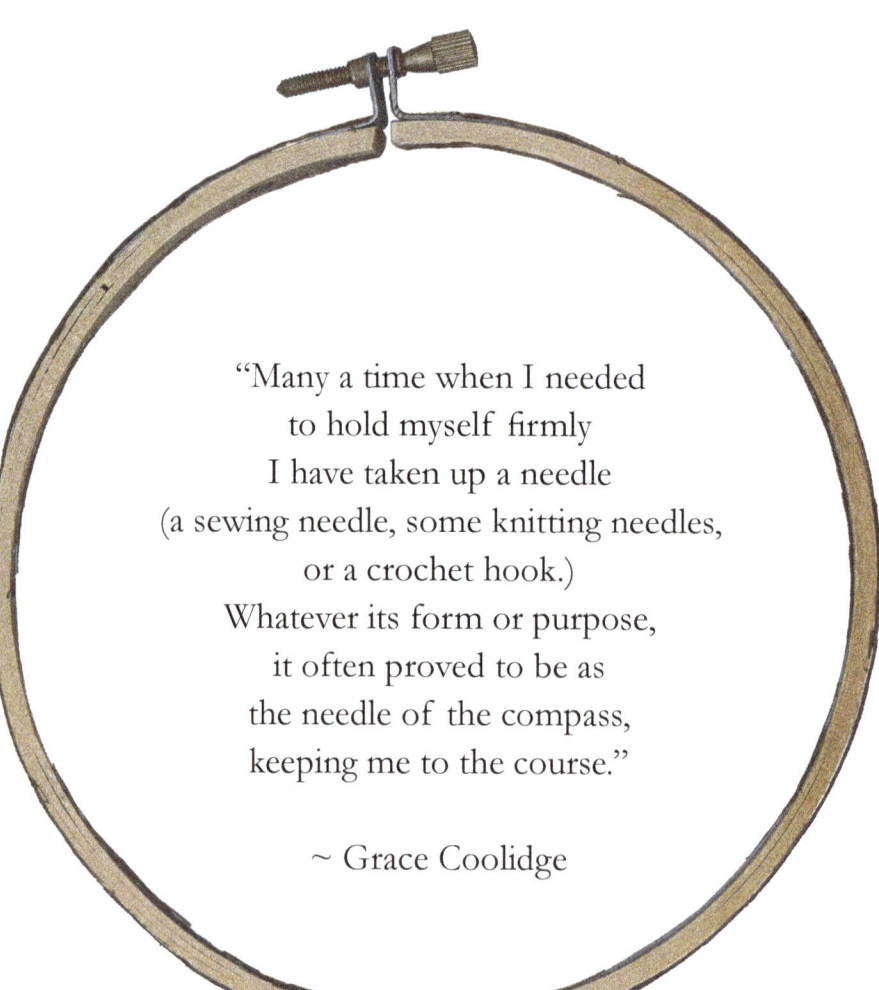

"Many a time when I needed
to hold myself firmly
I have taken up a needle
(a sewing needle, some knitting needles,
or a crochet hook.)
Whatever its form or purpose,
it often proved to be as
the needle of the compass,
keeping me to the course."

~ Grace Coolidge

www.ingramcontent.com/pod-product-compliance
Lightning Source LLC
Chambersburg PA
CBHW061128170426
43209CB00014B/1703